The Kids Book of
BLACK CANADIAN
HISTORY

WRITTEN BY

Rosemary Sadlier

ILLUSTRATED BY

Wang Qijun

KIDS CAN PRESS

To my parents, Henry and Bernice, for connecting me to Black Canadian history
through their living it and sharing it with me.

To my husband Jay and our three children, Jenne, Raia and Alexander,
for their encouragement and inspiration.

Acknowledgments
Many thanks to the Ontario Black History Society for the opportunity to use
their Black historical resources, and to Paul Braithwaite for his tireless efforts to critique this book.
Thank you to Donald Carty for the use of his archival materials and photographs.

I am greatly indebted to Elizabeth MacLeod for her patience and editing expertise, and to
Wang Qijun for his amazing artwork. Others to be thanked include Rivka Cranley, Kellie Cullihall,
Christine McClymont, Julia Naimska and all the dedicated people at Kids Can Press.

Photo credits
Page 28: poster courtesy Canadian Heritage. **Page 30:** stamp courtesy Canada Post.
Page 36: poster from National Archives of Canada/C-030621. **Page 38:** original of newspaper article
in collection of Glenbow Archives in Calgary (Photo/NA-3556-3b).

Text © 2003 Rosemary Sadlier
Illustrations © 2003 Wang Qijun

Kids Can Press acknowledges the financial support of the Ontario Arts Council, the Canada Council for the Arts
and the Government of Canada, through the BPIDP, for our publishing activity.

Published in Canada by
Kids Can Press Ltd.
29 Birch Avenue
Toronto, ON M4V 1E2

Published in the U.S. by
Kids Can Press Ltd.
2250 Military Road
Tonawanda, NY 14150

www.kidscanpress.com

Edited by Elizabeth MacLeod
Designed by Julia Naimska

Printed and bound in Hong Kong, China

This book is smyth sewn casebound.

CM 03 0 9 8 7 6 5 4 3 2 1

National Library of Canada Cataloguing in Publication Data

Sadlier, Rosemary
The kids book of Black Canadian history / written by Rosemary Sadlier ; illustrated by Wang Qijun.

Includes index.
ISBN 1-55074-892-0

1. Black Canadians — History — Juvenile literature. I. Wang Qijun II. Title.

FC106.B6S22 2003   305.896'071   C2002-905640-3
F1035.N3S22 2003

Kids Can Press is a Corus™ Entertainment company

CONTENTS

WHAT IS BLACK CANADIAN HISTORY?

Canada is one of the most diverse countries in the world. The people of Canada come from many different backgrounds — African, Chinese, Scottish, Ukrainian, Native peoples and hundreds more. Canadian history includes the stories of all these people.

But for a long time, history books focused only on White people from Great Britain and France. That's probably because these countries were the first to explore Canada, send settlers and keep records of their voyages. But the Native peoples were already here when these Europeans arrived.

What about Black people? The first arrived in Canada about 400 years ago. Black Canadians — also called African Canadians — have changed Canada and made important contributions to its story. They have a fascinating history full of strong, courageous people.

Why Did Black People Come to Canada?

Some Black people arrived in Canada as explorers. Many came to escape slavery. Others were soldiers who helped Britain defend Canada against the French or Americans. Still more hoped to fulfill their dreams or find a place where they could live, raise their families and work or go to school.

Where Black Canadians Were Born

Caribbean and Guyana (South America)	300 000 people
Africa	170 000 people
Canada and United States	110 000 people
TOTAL	**580 000 people**

Quick Facts

Black Canadians in Canada

Total population of Canada: 28 500 000

Number of Black people living in Canada: 580 000

Percentage of Canadian population that's Black: 2%

Percentage of the Black Canadian population living in:

Toronto	*47%*
Montreal	*20%*
Vancouver	*3%*
Nova Scotia	*3%*

Richard Pierpoint was a military hero who formed an all-Black regiment to fight in the War of 1812.

Mary Ann Shadd was the first female newspaper publisher in North America.

Josiah Henson founded the Dawn Settlement near Windsor, Ontario.

Harriet Tubman, a conductor on the Underground Railroad, saved more than 300 enslaved Black people.

African Roots

Whether their skin tone is light or dark, all Black people have African ancestors. Some Black Canadians have parents, grandparents and more ancestors who were born in Canada, while others have come recently from Africa, Bermuda, Europe, South America, the United States or Caribbean countries such as Barbados, Haiti, Jamaica or Trinidad.

Who Are the Black Canadians?

The four main groups of Black Canadians are:

• People who have lived in Canada for several generations
• Immigrants from Bermuda, the Caribbean and South America
• Immigrants from Africa
• Immigrants from the United States
   Most people in the first group originally came from the United States. But Black Canadians all share a common African heritage. Today, they feel a connection to one another through their experiences of life in Canada.

Time to Tell the Story

For years, Canadians didn't see Black Canadians in history books, on television or in newspapers — their story wasn't told. Many people, Black or White, didn't know about Black people's important contributions to Canada. But Black Canadians have added to Canada's story in many ways. From military heroes and journalists to cowboys and activists, Black Canadians have a proud history, present and future.

Carrie Best, a journalist, fought for equal rights for Black citizens.

Dr. Anderson Ruffin Abbott was the first Black graduate of Toronto's Medical College.

The seven Carty brothers from New Brunswick fought in World War II.

AFRICAN BEGINNINGS

Black Canadian history started on the continent of Africa. Like Canada, Africa is a diverse place. Most African people are Black, but others are of Asian, Arab and European descent. Africa is made up of many countries, and its people have a great number of religions, languages, foods and traditions.

Africa's history is interesting and long. The oldest known human being lived 2 million years ago in Africa. From this African birthplace, humans spread out to all parts of the world, including, eventually, Canada.

About Africa

- *Africa is the second-largest continent in the world.*

- *Africa is three times the size of Canada.*

- *The total population of Africa is about 700 million people.*

- *There are 52 countries in Africa.*

- *Between 800 and 1000 languages are spoken in Africa.*

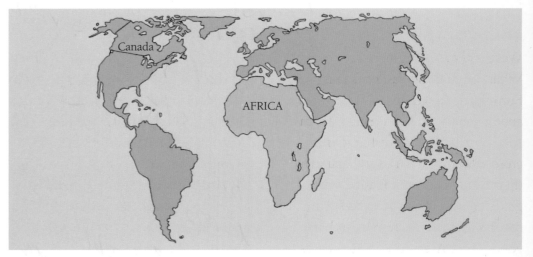

Beginning in Africa

Long before the European explorers arrived in Africa, it had great cities and powerful empires. The African people were skilled farmers, doctors, merchants, metal-workers and sailors. They traded with the Arabs to the north and the Indians to the east. For thousands of years, they'd also been creating wonderful art.

Most people know about the amazing civilization of ancient Egypt, in northeastern Africa. It began more than 5000 years ago along the Nile River. You can still visit the pyramids, which are the tombs of Egyptian kings or pharaohs. But there were other incredible civilizations in Africa.

The Kingdom of Kush

Kush became a kingdom in Nubia, on the Nile River south of Egypt, around 800 B.C.E. The Kushites conquered Egypt and ruled it for about 100 years. Kush continued to flourish until 300 C.E.

The Kushites were wealthy and inventive. They built pyramids, trained elephants to work and made iron tools and weapons while the Egyptians were still using bronze, a softer metal. They also developed the world's first form of writing based on an alphabet.

Religion in Africa

From the earliest times, African tribes had their own religions. The people believed they were surrounded by spirits of nature and of their ancestors. Using songs, drumming, dances and other rituals, they asked the spirits for protection.

About 2000 years ago, Christianity came to Africa. Then, 700 years later, Islam arrived in North Africa. Over the centuries, it replaced Christianity in most parts of Africa except Ethiopia. Many African kings and their people became Muslims, or believers in Islam. But the older African religions survived alongside the newer religions.

At Lalibela, a mountain village in Ethiopia, ten Christian churches were carved out of solid rock during the 13th century.

West African Kingdoms

While knights and castles flourished in Europe, the kingdoms of Ghana, Mali and Songhay arose in western Africa.

Traders from these kingdoms crossed the Sahara Desert regularly, their camel caravans loaded with gold and salt. They returned carrying metal, cloth and leather goods from Arab countries such as Morocco, in northern Africa. With the wealth gained from trade, Ghana, Mali and Songhay built beautiful cities. Their kings received visitors in splendid palaces.

Mansa Kankan Musa

In 1324, Mansa Kankan Musa, a wealthy king of Mali, made a pilgrimage to the sacred Muslim city of Mecca. He was accompanied by 60 000 people and 100 camels loaded with gold. While visiting Cairo in Egypt, he gave away so much gold that it lost its value. The price of gold stayed low for the next 12 years!

"IT IS A WONDER TO SEE WHAT PLENTY OF MERCHANDISE IS DAILY BROUGHT HITHER, AND HOW COSTLY AND SUMPTUOUS ALL THINGS BE."

— *Leo Africanus, a Spaniard visiting Songhay in 1510*

East African dhows *designed to sail against the wind*

East African Trading Cities

The Swahilis of East Africa built stone cities 1000 years ago on the coast of the Indian Ocean — Mogadishu (in Somalia), Mombasa (in Kenya) and Kilwa (on an island off Tanzania).

Traders sailed from these cities in ships called *dhows*. They carried cargoes of iron goods to China and India and returned with cotton cloth, porcelain and copper. Farther south, Zimbabwe was also an important trading power.

DID YOU KNOW

Timbuktu in Mali had an important Muslim university at least 600 years ago. Students from as far away as Europe went there to study astronomy, literature, mathematics, medicine and music.

The Great Zimbabwe was built in the 1300s. Although today it is in ruins, it was once the residence of a powerful ruler.

7

THE ATLANTIC SLAVE TRADE

In 1498, Vasco da Gama, an explorer from Portugal, became the first European to sail around Africa. With great excitement, he discovered some of Africa's wealthy cities. After his voyage, trade between Africa and Europe increased rapidly. Portugal, Britain and other countries wanted to trade for African gold, silk and ivory.

A small trade in slaves began as well. At that time, slavery was common around the world. Slaves were usually criminals or prisoners of war and could be of any race. In Africa, enslaved people were used as workers in salt mines and as porters on trade caravans. But according to law, these African slaves could purchase their freedom after some years.

Plantations of the New World

In 1492, Christopher Columbus sailed across the Atlantic Ocean from Spain and landed on a Caribbean island. He thought he had reached the Far East. Instead, his search for gold and spices had led him to discover a "New World." Of course, it wasn't a new world to the Native peoples who lived there.

The tropical climate of the islands gave the Spanish an idea. In order to profit from Columbus's "mistake," they set up huge farms, called plantations, to grow sugar cane there. These plantations needed many workers, so the Spanish owners forced the Native people to work as slaves. But many of the slaves fled or died from European diseases such as smallpox and measles.

By 1600, the Portuguese, British, French and Dutch also had plantations and mines in the Caribbean and the Americas. They all needed workers, and so they turned to the slave traders. In Africa, both Africans and Europeans rounded up men and women and marched them in chains to coastal cities. There they were crammed into ships and sent across the Atlantic Ocean. The Atlantic slave trade became a huge business.

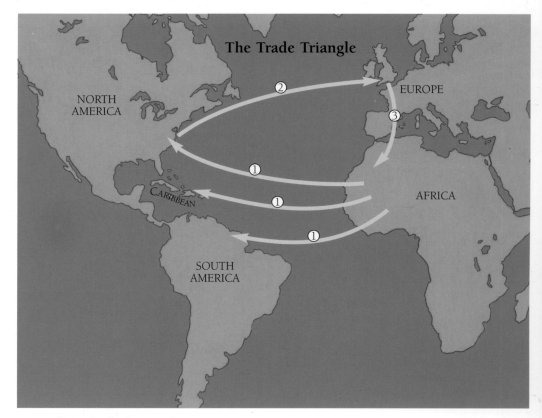

The Trade Triangle

1. **Enslaved Black people are shipped from Africa to New World colonies in the Caribbean and the Americas.**
2. **Products such as sugar and gold are sent from the colonies back to Europe.**
3. **Manufactured goods such as guns and cotton cloth are sent to Africa in trade for the slaves.**

DID YOU KNOW

During the Atlantic slave trade, some British slaving ships were built in Newfoundland, although enslaved Black people were never brought directly to Britain's northern colonies.

The Slave Ships

Conditions on the slave ships were hideous. Before boarding, the captives were branded like cattle so that their purchasers could identify them on arrival. Once on board, they were packed in so closely they could barely move. Afraid of revolts, sailors guarded the slaves with guns. There were terrible shortages of drinking water and food during the voyage. Many enslaved people became sick and died.

THE CAPTIVES "… WERE ALL ENCLOSED UNDER GRATED HATCHWAYS BETWEEN DECKS. THE SPACE WAS SO LOW THAT THEY SAT BETWEEN EACH OTHERS' LEGS, AND STOWED SO CLOSE TOGETHER, THAT THERE WAS NO POSSIBILITY OF LYING DOWN, OR AT ALL CHANGING THEIR POSITIONS, BY NIGHT OR BY DAY."

— *report from a British anti-slaving patrol in 1829*

Effects of the Slave Trade

The Atlantic slave trade lasted 250 years, from about 1600 to 1850. At least 20 million Black people were taken from Africa to the Americas, the Caribbean, China, Europe and other countries. Historians say that 10 to 12 million captives landed alive in the Americas and Caribbean. Almost one-third of all Black people died during the passage.

The effect on Africa was devastating, as communities lost their strongest young people and most educated adults. The New World gained from the skills the Africans brought with them, including their knowledge of tropical agriculture, healing and carpentry. Others contributed music and other arts to the culture of their new home.

◆ PROFILE ◆

ABU BAKR AL-SIDDIQ

Most enslaved Africans who crossed the Atlantic Ocean never saw their homes again. Abu Bakr al-Siddiq was an exception. Born in Timbuktu in 1790, he was brought up in a well-educated Muslim family, then captured and sent to Jamaica as a slave. There, his master discovered that he could read and write Arabic (like many other enslaved people). As a result, al-Siddiq was freed after 30 years of slavery. He joined an English expedition to Timbuktu and managed to return home.

SLAVERY IN NEW FRANCE

While the Atlantic slave trade was growing, Europeans were exploring the northern parts of North America. John Cabot, who was born in Italy (where he was known as Giovanni Caboto), sailed to Canada's east coast from Bristol, England, in 1497.

After Cabot's voyage, Britain claimed ownership of North America. But another 100 years passed before Britain founded its first colony, Virginia, in what's now the United States. Then, in 1608, the explorer Samuel de Champlain established a colony for France at what is now Quebec City. Over the next 150 years, this colony — New France — grew, and its population reached about 65 000.

NEW FRANCE

Who Were the Slaves?

The first slaves in New France were people of the Pawnee Nation, called *panis* by the French. But many of the Native slaves were killed by European diseases. So the French settlers imported African slaves from American and Caribbean plantations. These slaves had built up immunity to most European diseases. Plus, because of their dark skin colour, it was harder for them to blend in with the people around them if they ran away.

There weren't many enslaved Black people in New France, however. The long, cold winters prevented the settlers from creating large plantations like the ones in the southern colonies. Their small farms didn't need huge numbers of workers.

New France's First Black Slave

The first enslaved African in New France was a young boy. He was born on the island of Madagascar, off Africa's east coast. At age seven, he was sold as a slave to the British commander David Kirke. When Kirke invaded Quebec City in 1628, he sold the boy to the colony's head clerk, Olivier LeTardif.

New France was handed back to the French in 1632. LeTardif had to flee because he had worked for the British, but he sold his young slave first. The boy was educated in a school run by a Jesuit priest, Father Le Jeune. Later, the enslaved boy was baptized Olivier Le Jeune — his first name came from Olivier

DID YOU KNOW

Although slavery wasn't legal in France, the Code Noir (Black Code) made it acceptable in New France. Passed by King Louis XIV of France, the Black Code stated how slaves were to be treated. Owners couldn't marry their slaves, and the children of slaves were the property of the slave owner. Slavery was made fully legal in New France in 1709.

LeTardif and his last name from Father Le Jeune. Olivier Le Jeune died when he was 30.

Slave Labour

The living conditions for enslaved people in New France were less harsh than on the plantations in the South. Most slaves lived in the cities of Montreal and Quebec and worked in people's houses as domestic servants. They washed and ironed clothes, cooked meals and cared for children. Some of the men worked as farm labourers.

Things were different outside the cities, however, where heavy outdoor work was needed. For example, enslaved Black people helped to build and protect French fur-trading posts.

All sorts of people were slave owners — military men, merchants, governors and priests. Even Catholic women's convents used slave labour in their hospitals and schools.

Enslaved people were at the lowest level of society. Their owners could beat them whenever they wished. Many died young, at an average age of 25. By 1760, New France's population of 65 000 included about 1200 Black slaves and 2500 *panis*.

Marie-Joseph Angélique

The story of Marie-Joseph Angélique shows how harshly slaves could be punished. Angélique was a house slave in Montreal. In April 1734, she learned that she was about to be sold and decided to run away. While she was escaping, a fire started in her owner's house. The flames spread and destroyed 46 homes. When Angélique was captured, she was found guilty of starting the fire, tortured, paraded through the streets and hanged.

◆ PROFILE ◆

MATHIEU DA COSTA

The first Black person known to have come to Canada (as the country would later be called) was a free man, not a slave. Sometime before 1605, Mathieu Da Costa travelled from France to the new French colony of Port Royal, in today's Nova Scotia.

Da Costa was a translator — he could speak French as well as the language of the local Native people, the Mi'kmaq. The French needed Da Costa to help them trade with the Mi'kmaq. As a member of the Order of Good Cheer, Canada's first social club, Da Costa also took his turn with the other men in putting on shows or providing other entertainment for the club. He returned to Europe around 1607.

ISSUE: SLAVERY

A slave is a human being who is the property of another person. In the slave trade, people were bought and sold like cattle at a farm market.

In the past, slavery was common in many countries. For instance, White Europeans enslaved other White Europeans, and some Native Canadians had slaves. If you were taken prisoner in a battle, or if you owed someone a lot of money, you might be made a slave. Usually, slaves could work hard and purchase their freedom. Slavery didn't necessarily last for a lifetime.

When Africans were captured and shipped to the New World, however, things changed. The Africans were enslaved for their entire lives, and their children were the owner's property. There was no way they could buy their freedom. For these Black people, slavery was a permanent condition.

African Culture in the New World

In the Caribbean and South America, enslaved Black people far outnumbered White people. As a result, they were able to keep alive their African songs, languages and religions. In the United States, however, much of African culture was soon forgotten by the children and grandchildren of the enslaved Black people. Canada had only a small population of slaves, and their heritage also was mostly forgotten.

American Plantations

A plantation is a large farm that grows one crop, such as cotton, sugar or coffee. Most plantations are in tropical countries or places with hot climates, such as the southern United States. Plantation owners needed many workers. Most owned 10 to 20 enslaved Blacks, but some of the richer ones had 100 or more. Because slaves were forced to work for free, the owners could make large profits.

The enslaved Africans who lived on American plantations had a harsh life. As slaves, they had no rights. They weren't allowed to go to school or learn to read and write, nor could they legally marry or go anywhere without their owner's permission. As well, slaves were punished or sold whenever their owner liked.

Work of a Field Slave

Most male and many female slaves toiled in the fields. They worked 16-hour days, from sunrise to sundown, six days a week. Supervised by overseers — White men or trusted slaves — they hoed, planted or harvested crops under the hot sun. If an enslaved person arrived late, made a mistake or worked too slowly, he could receive 50 to 100 lashes from the overseer's whip.

Other Slave Work

About one-quarter of enslaved Black people were house slaves or tradespeople such as carpenters, builders and weavers. House slaves worked in the "big house," performing tasks for the owner's wife and family. Most were children, women or old people, and they worked as cooks, caregivers, grooms and drivers. They had to do whatever their owner demanded. If they angered the owner, they could be whipped.

Family Life

Slave families lived together in small cabins away from the owner's house. They often had six or seven children, who had to begin working when they were just 7 or 8 years old.

The more fortunate families had garden plots and could grow their own food. They also hunted and fished to get enough to eat. Singing, dancing, storytelling and practising their religion helped keep their culture alive. Sundays were free, and Christmas brought a few days' holiday.

JOSIAH HENSON

Josiah Henson was born enslaved in Maryland in 1789. When he was about 3, his father tried to protect his mother from a savage beating. For this crime, his father had an ear cut off, was whipped and sold to a new owner.

Henson and his mother were purchased by a Kentucky farmer called Isaac Riley. Henson was such a reliable worker that, when he grew up, he was made manager of Riley's farm.

While still enslaved, Henson became a Christian preacher. But the cruelty of slavery made him increasingly angry. When he was 20, a savage beating broke both his shoulders. Two years later, Henson married a young enslaved woman named Charlotte and started a family. He began to think about escaping.

Henson finally made his break for freedom in 1830 after Riley betrayed him. He and Charlotte and their children set out on a long, terrifying journey from Kentucky. (Read more about Henson on pages 25 and 30.)

Religion on the Plantations

For the first 100 years of slavery, White owners didn't want their enslaved workers to become Christians. But by the mid-1700s, many Black people began to join Protestant churches, especially Baptist and Methodist. Soon, Black people were turning church services into joyous occasions full of music and movement.

Some plantation owners tried to control slaves through religion. They would bring a White Christian minister to preach to the enslaved people. The message? That obedience to the owner was a good thing, and slaves should be happy to be slaves.

But the slaves understood Christianity in a different way. In the Bible, they read about the Jewish slaves in Egypt. They believed that God had sent Moses to free the Jews from their masters, and they longed for the same freedom.

Spirituals

In their religious songs, called spirituals, the slaves sang about their hopes of becoming free or going to heaven. Later, when the slaves were escaping to Canada, these songs contained coded messages to help them travel the Underground Railroad (see page 24).

Let My People Go

When Israel was in Egypt's land,
Let my people go,
Oppressed so hard they could not stand,
Let my people go.

Go down, Moses,
Way down in Egypt land,
Tell ole Pharaoh,
Let my people go.

The Auction Block

In their lifetime, most enslaved people would live on two or more plantations. When an owner decided to sell some slaves, he took them to a market, where they were closely examined by purchasers. Some owners employed a slave trader to help them sell their slaves. The trader would feed the enslaved Blacks just enough so that they looked healthy at sale time.

It was common for slave families to be split up when sold. Children were separated from parents, and husbands from wives. Often, they never saw one another again. Enslaved people who were moving to a new plantation marched in "coffles" — lines of people chained together. Many died before they arrived.

Slave auctions were frequent in Canada as well, especially in Nova Scotia. In the 1700s, newspapers regularly advertised sales of skilled slaves.

TO BE SOLD,
A BLACK WOMAN, named PEGGY, aged about forty years ; and a Black boy her son, named JUPITER, aged about fifteen years, both of them the property of the Subscriber.

The Woman is a tolerable Cook and washer woman and perfectly understands making Soap and Candles.

The Boy is tall and strong of his age, and has been employed in Country business, but brought up principally as a House Servant—They are each of them Servants for life. The Price for the Woman is one hundred and fifty Dollars—for the Boy two hundred Dollars, payable in three years with Interest from the day of Sale and to be properly secured by Bond &c.— But one fourth less will be taken in ready Money.

PETER RUSSELL.

York, Feb. 10th 1806.

WHEN I WAS 15 YEARS OLD, I WAS BROUGHT TO THE COURTHOUSE, PUT UP ON THE AUCTION BLOCK TO BE SOLD. OLD JUDGE MILLER WAS THERE. I KNEW HIM WELL BECAUSE HE WAS ONE OF THE WEALTHIEST SLAVE OWNERS IN THE COUNTY AND THE MEANEST ONE ... I SPOKE RIGHT OUT ON THE AUCTION BLOCK AND TOLD HIM: "JUDGE MILLER! DON'T YOU BID FOR ME, 'CAUSE IF YOU DO, I WOULD NOT LIVE ON YOUR PLANTATION. I WILL TAKE A KNIFE AND CUT MY OWN THROAT FROM EAR TO EAR BEFORE I WOULD BE OWNED BY YOU."

— *Delicia Patterson, an enslaved Black American girl*

In 1831, Nat Turner, a slave from Virginia, led a slave revolt during which more than 60 White people were killed. Soldiers were called in to stop the rebellion. The incident led to harsher laws in the American South that restricted the movement of enslaved people. As a result, many enslaved people tried to escape to Canada — by that time, slavery was illegal here.

Slave Life in Canada

Most enslaved Black people in early Canada were house slaves. Besides cleaning the owner's house, doing the laundry and preparing meals, they cared for children and old people, made clothing, candles and soap, and tended small vegetable gardens. Some developed trades such as carpentry, blacksmithing and hairdressing. Others helped to clear the land, chop logs and store firewood in preparation for the long, cold winters.

The Fight Against Slavery

There were always people who objected to slavery. They were called abolitionists because they wanted to end, or abolish, slavery. One group was the Quakers in the northern American colonies. Quakers were Christians who felt that all people deserved liberty in the eyes of God.

In Britain, too, there were strong opponents to slavery, such as William Wilberforce, a Member of Parliament. In Upper Canada (now Ontario), Lieutenant-Governor John Graves Simcoe took a big step towards abolishing slavery in 1793 (see page 17).

After Slavery

When the Civil War broke out in the United States in 1861, many slaves in the South escaped to fight for the North. Two years later, President Abraham Lincoln signed the Emancipation Proclamation, making slavery illegal in the U.S. After the North won the war in 1865, all American slaves were declared free, although many slave owners tried to hide the news from their enslaved people.

Slavery still exists today in China, some African countries and elsewhere. Often the slaves are poor children who are purchased from their parents.

SLAVERY IN BRITISH CANADA

About 250 years ago, in 1763, France lost its "Seven Years' War" with Britain, and New France became a British colony called Quebec. For Black and Native slaves, little changed under British rule. Enslaved people were still considered the property of their owners and had no rights of their own.

General James Murray, the first British governor of Quebec, was a slave owner. So were several other government officials. Many more enslaved Black people would arrive in British Canada and several decades would pass before slavery ended.

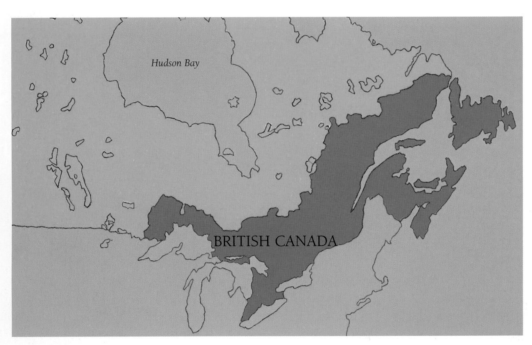

Nova Scotia and Prince Edward Island

Nova Scotia became a British colony in 1749. Settlers arriving from New England brought slaves with them, and Black slaves helped to build the city of Halifax. By 1767, there were more than 100 slaves in Nova Scotia. Newspapers such as the *Nova Scotia Advertiser* and the *Royal Gazette* advertised slave auctions and published notices offering rewards for runaways.

A much smaller number of slaves lived in the colony of Isle St. Jean (which became Prince Edward Island in 1799). Two enslaved Black people came with a merchant from New York. A few more were owned by Colonel Joseph Robinson from North Carolina. Slavery continued in Prince Edward Island until 1825.

> "BLACK SLAVES ARE CERTAINLY THE ONLY PEOPLE TO BE DEPENDED UPON, BUT IT IS NECESSARY, I IMAGINE, THEY SHOULD BE BORN IN ONE OR OTHER OF OUR NORTHERN COLONIES, THE WINTERS HERE WILL NOT AGREE WITH A NATIVE OF THE TORRID ZONE ..."
>
> — *General James Murray*

Upper Canada

In 1791, Britain divided the enormous Province of Quebec into Lower Canada (now Quebec) and Upper Canada (now Ontario). At that time, there were still enslaved Black people living in both colonies. The man who governed Upper Canada from 1796, Peter Russell, was a slave owner.

Another slave owner in Upper Canada was Joseph Brant. He was a famous Mohawk chief who was loyal to Britain during the American Revolution (also called the War of American Independence). As a reward, Brant received a large grant of land in what's now southwestern Ontario. He owned about 30 slaves, but he also allowed free Black people to live on his land and marry people in his tribe.

Joseph Brant's carriage driver may have been one of his Black slaves.

Justifying Slavery

It's hard to understand how one group of people could enslave another. When the African slave trade began, many European people felt guilty about the way they were treating their captives. They and some White settlers in the colonies tried to justify the slave trade. Many felt that it was permissible because it made them money. Others argued that the Africans were uncivilized savages and — even worse — pagans (not Christians).

But most enslaved Black people became Christians in the New World. Then White Christians who supported slavery looked in the Bible for new arguments. Some claimed that Black people were the descendants of Ham, one of Noah's sons, whom Noah condemned to be a servant. (Noah was the man in the Bible who obeyed God's order to build an ark. He loaded two of every species of animal onto this ship and escaped a great flood.)

Such false theories of Black inferiority led to racism, which still persists.

JOHN GRAVES SIMCOE

John Graves Simcoe was the Lieutenant-Governor, or leader, of Upper Canada from 1792 to 1796. Born in England, Simcoe was good at sports and popular in school. After joining the army, he was sent overseas to fight as a British commander during the American Revolution. Later, in the British Parliament, Simcoe spoke out against slavery.

When Simcoe settled in Newark (now Niagara-on-the-Lake), in Upper Canada, he was shocked to hear about the case of Chloë Cooley, an enslaved Black girl from nearby Queenston. Cooley had been tied up by her master, thrown into a boat and taken across the Niagara River to the United States to be sold.

Simcoe's government quickly passed a law, in 1793, to limit slavery. The law said that any child born to a slave in Upper Canada would become free at age 25, and that no new slaves could be brought into the province. After this, slavery slowly began to disappear in Upper Canada.

DID YOU KNOW

In 1777, Vermont became the first British colony to abolish slavery. Some enslaved people from Quebec escaped there to freedom. It was almost 100 years later that President Lincoln abolished slavery across the United States.

BLACK LOYALISTS IN THE MARITIMES

In 1775, a war broke out in America that brought many new people — Black and White — to Britain's east-coast Canadian colonies, the Maritimes.

The Thirteen Colonies in America, discontented with British rule, were battling for their independence.

After a long and bitter struggle, the Americans won the American Revolution in 1783. This led to the founding of the United States of America. But while many Americans were celebrating the birth of the United States, thousands of others were leaving for a new life in Canada.

Canada — A Safe Haven

During the American Revolution, Canada became known as a safe place for Black people. Slavery still existed, but the British promised freedom and land in Canada to all Black people who fought on their side in the war. They did this because they needed allies. Also, the British wanted to ensure that the Canadian colonies wouldn't join the Americans in their fight for independence.

Attracted by the British offer, thousands of enslaved people ran away from their plantation masters and joined up.

Black Loyalists

Americans who stayed loyal to Britain during the Revolution were called United Empire Loyalists. After Britain's defeat, 30 000 Loyalists gathered in New York and set sail for Nova Scotia. About 3500 were Black people who had been given their freedom. Another 1500 were Black slaves brought by White Loyalists.

Looking forward to a new life, most of the free Black Loyalists settled in Nova Scotia and New Brunswick. Others travelled to Upper and Lower Canada.

Birchtown

In 1784, Birchtown was the largest free Black town outside of Africa, with a population of more than 1500 people.

Despite being overcrowded, Birchtown developed a strong community life. Like other Maritime Black people, Birchtown residents often gathered to work, visit or attend church services.

DID YOU KNOW

Birchtown was named after General Samuel Birch. Birch was the British officer who protected the Black Loyalists in New York after the American Revolution and signed most of their Certificates of Freedom.

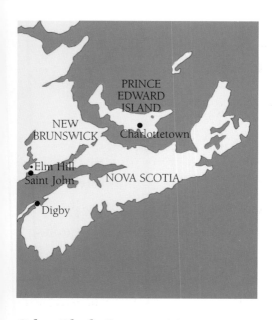

Other Black Communities

Black settlements were built outside other towns in the Maritimes because that's where Black people were given land. Preston and Digby, in Nova Scotia, and Charlottetown, in Prince Edward Island, had Black settlements similar to Birchtown. Near Saint John, New Brunswick, Black people established small centres such as Loch Lomond and Elm Hill.

Churches

Churches — Baptist, Methodist, Anglican and Catholic — were a big part of life for Black Loyalists in Nova Scotia. British and Canadian charitable groups helped build and support Black churches. David George, a Black activist and reformer, built Baptist churches all over Nova Scotia using money the Black community donated.

Waiting for Land

Many Black Loyalists waited up to five years for the land they'd been promised. If they did receive it, their plots were half the size offered to the White people. The soil was thin and rocky, and farming was very difficult.

In Birchtown, community leaders Thomas Peters and Murphy Still protested the long waits. Both men were former Black Pioneers. Perhaps for that reason, they succeeded in getting land for themselves. But many Black settlers never received the farms that had been promised to them.

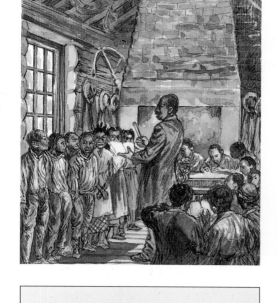

Schools and Self-Help

British charities also assisted with the building of schools in Black communities. Colonel Blucke became a teacher at one of these schools in Birchtown. He hoped that education would enable his people to prosper.

Inspired by activists such as David George, Black people formed self-help organizations and anti-slavery groups. Much later, in the 1960s, these groups would join the civil rights movement, which began in the United States, to demand equal rights for all Black people.

Disappointment

Black Loyalists who had no land were forced to work for White farmers or merchants to earn money. They were poor, mistreated and even denied the right to vote. Birchtown and other Black communities began to look like refugee camps rather than successful towns.

◆ PROFILE ◆

THE BLACK PIONEERS

The only all-Black British regiment in the American Revolution was the Black Pioneers. In the army, a pioneer was a soldier who did tasks including clearing ground for camps, removing obstructions and digging trenches. Black men weren't permitted to serve as regular soldiers.

After the war, the Black Pioneers settled in Nova Scotia. They helped to design and build the town of Shelburne. Many White Loyalists moved there, but the land grants the Pioneers and their leader, Colonel Stephen Blucke, received were located outside of Shelburne. There, they built Birchtown, where other Black Loyalists soon joined them.

BACK TO AFRICA

Many Black Loyalists were unhappy in the Maritimes. They were frustrated by the lack of decent land and work. When a message of hope came, they were ready for it. That message came in 1791 from Thomas Peters, a former Black Pioneer. Peters had sailed from Nova Scotia to England to complain to the British government about the Black Loyalists' situation.

While in London, Peters met members of an anti-slavery organization. They were looking for Black settlers to form a new colony in Africa. When Peters returned to Birchtown, he and an Englishman, Lieutenant John Clarkson, convinced many people that this would be a good opportunity. So, in January 1792, 1200 of the original Black Loyalists — more than one-third — sailed for Sierra Leone. Most had never seen Africa before.

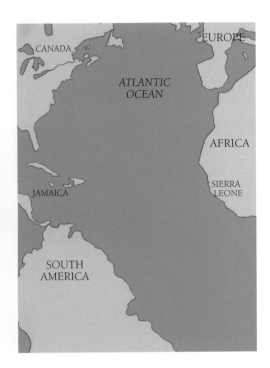

Sierra Leone

Sierra Leone is a small West African country. Granville Sharp, a British abolitionist, established a colony there in 1787 for 2000 freed slaves from Britain and America. Others joined them, including some Africans rescued from slave ships and the Nova Scotian Black Loyalists. Conditions in Sierra Leone were difficult — food was scarce and local people were unfriendly — but the Black Canadians never returned to Canada. (Sierra Leone remained under British control until 1961, then became an independent country.)

The Jamaican Maroons

The Maritimes were about to receive other Black immigrants. In Jamaica, a group of fearless Black fighters had been frustrating the British for years. The Maroons were African slaves who had escaped from the Spanish in the 1600s. From their mountain hideouts, they fought off attackers for 100 years.

The British conquered Jamaica in the early 1700s, but they couldn't conquer the Maroons. Like guerrilla fighters, the Maroons launched surprise raids, then disappeared into the mountains. But in 1795, with the help of vicious attack dogs, the British tricked them into surrendering. One year later, the British government transported 600 Maroons to their new home — the colony of Nova Scotia.

DID YOU KNOW

"Maroon," the name for a fugitive slave, may come from the Spanish-American word *cimarron*, which means "living on the mountaintops."

NANNY OF THE MAROONS

Nanny is a national hero in Jamaica. A fearless warrior, she led the Maroons in their fight against the British in the early 1700s. Nanny was a small, wiry woman with piercing eyes. The legends say that she was especially skilled in planning sneak attacks to catch her enemies off guard.

Nanny was also a wise woman of her village. She encouraged her people to preserve the customs, music and songs they had brought from Africa. Even after Nanny died in 1734, her love of freedom encouraged Black Jamaicans to continue their struggle towards independence.

On to Sierra Leone

Finally, the Maroon colonel, Montague James, petitioned the government to save his people from their "miserable situation" and send them to a warmer climate. To back up the demand, the Maroons refused to work.

The British and Nova Scotian governments considered their options. The money from Jamaica was running out, and conflicts were still simmering between the Maroons and other Halifax residents. It was decided that the Maroons would go to Sierra Leone, and in August 1800, 550 of them set sail for Africa. They never returned to Canada.

The Maroons in Nova Scotia

When the Maroons arrived in Halifax in 1796, stories of their bravery circulated around the town. Nova Scotia's Governor Wentworth welcomed them, saying they added cheerfulness and energy to the colony. He made sure the newcomers had places to live and put them to work constructing a fortress called the Citadel. At first, both jobs and housing were paid for by the Jamaican government.

Over the next four years, things went wrong. The local people disliked the Maroons' independent spirit and disapproved of their "un-Christian" ways. Since the Maroons were given jobs, homes and provisions, the locals also felt the Maroons got better treatment than they did. The Maroons, in turn, disliked the cold climate and poor food. They got frostbite the first winter and couldn't grow their favourite crops of yams, bananas, cocoa and peppers.

Belongings of a Maroon

The British government gave these provisions to one Maroon family, Major and Mrs. John Jarrett and their daughter, when they arrived in Halifax:

24 handkerchiefs, 2 coats, 21 blankets, 4 vests, 3 walking sticks, 1 box of trinkets, 1 pair of trousers, 16 gowns, 6 shirts, 15 petticoats, 4 pairs of stockings, 3 pairs of shoes, 2 men's hats, 2 women's hats, 2 towels, 1 tablecloth, bedding, miscellaneous.

THE COLORED CORPS

At the start of the 19th century, many American slaves longed to escape to Upper Canada. Ten years earlier, in 1793, the province's lieutenant-governor, John Graves Simcoe, had promised that any enslaved Black people who entered the province would be granted their freedom.

On plantations in the American South, worried owners tried to frighten their slaves with tales about the terrible things that would happen to them if they went to Canada. But a trickle of Black Americans began to make the difficult journey north. Upper Canada's small Black population, which still included about 1000 enslaved people, grew as the new arrivals put down roots.

Preparing for War

In the early 1800s, Black people in Upper Canada began to hear rumours of a new war between Britain and the United States. They feared that, if the Americans won, slavery would return to their province. So Richard Pierpoint, a Black Loyalist, made a plan to help defeat the Americans. In 1812, he wrote to the government asking to form an all-Black military unit to fight for Britain.

Permission was granted. The unit Pierpoint formed was put under the command of a White officer, Captain Robert Runchey, and was called Captain Runchey's Company of Colored Men, or the Colored Corps. The Black officers were Sergeants James Watters and Edward Gough, with Corporals Humphrey Waters, Francis Willson and William Thomas.

◆ PROFILE ◆

RICHARD PIERPOINT

Richard Pierpoint was a true Black Canadian hero. He was born in 1744 in Bondou, Senegal, Africa. At 16, he was captured by slave traders and sent to America. During the American Revolution, Pierpoint fought on the British side.

In 1780, Pierpoint settled near Niagara Falls and became one of Upper Canada's first pioneers. His Colored Corps was Canada's first all-Black military unit, starting a tradition that continued until World War II. When Pierpoint was an old man, he asked the government for money so that he could go home to Africa. Instead, he received a 40 ha (100 acre) farm along the Grand River (near Guelph, Ontario). He lived there, with a few other African families, until his death at the age of 94 in 1838.

Britain and the United States at War Again

In 1812, 30 years after winning the War of American Independence, the Americans declared war on Britain again. One of the main reasons was that the British, who were fighting France for control of the oceans, had stopped and searched American ships. The Americans began by attacking the closest British colonies — Upper and Lower Canada.

President Thomas Jefferson said that conquering Canada would be "a mere question of marching." He was wrong. Canadian soldiers — both Black and White — defended their country fiercely.

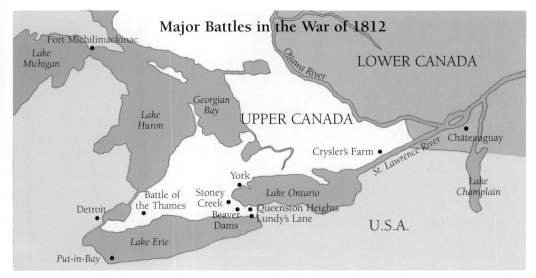

Major Battles in the War of 1812

Fort Michilimackinac
Lake Michigan
Lake Huron
Georgian Bay
Ottawa River
LOWER CANADA
UPPER CANADA
Crysler's Farm
St. Lawrence River
Châteauguay
York
Lake Ontario
Lake Champlain
Battle of the Thames
Stoney Creek
Beaver Dams
Queenston Heights
Lundy's Lane
Detroit
Lake Erie
U.S.A.
Put-in-Bay

Valour in Battle

The Colored Corps was a valued part of the British and Canadian forces and successfully fought the Americans in a number of battles. In Upper Canada, these included Fort George, Niagara Town, Stoney Creek and Lundy's Lane. The Corps also played an important role at Queenston Heights, the most famous battle of the war.

Many other Black volunteers fought with White military units. Thousands of American ex-slaves — promised freedom and land by the British — arrived to fight as well.

Who Won the War of 1812?

During the War of 1812, British and Canadian troops, joined by Black Americans and Native Canadian soldiers, captured several American forts, including Detroit, and burned the White House to the ground. However neither side won, and the war ended in a stalemate in 1814. But by fighting together to keep the Americans out, Canadians of all backgrounds began to feel a new sense of pride.

Near Niagara Falls, in Queenston Park, a national historic monument commemorates the achievements of the Colored Corps.

Black Veterans

After the war, the new lieutenant-governor of Upper Canada, Sir Peregrine Maitland, rewarded about 70 veterans of the Colored Corps with land in Oro township, near Barrie, Ontario. Maitland opposed slavery — he refused to return runaway slaves to their owners in the American South, and he stopped American slave hunters at the border.

Nova Scotia and New Brunswick offered Black war veterans freedom and protection, so about 2000 of them settled there. Many Black Maritimers are descendants of those American veterans.

"THAT YOUR EXCELLENCY'S PETITIONER IS NOW OLD AND WITHOUT PROPERTY; THAT HE FINDS IT DIFFICULT TO OBTAIN A LIVELIHOOD BY HIS LABOUR; THAT HE IS ABOVE ALL THINGS DESIROUS TO RETURN TO HIS NATIVE COUNTRY …"

— from Richard Pierpoint's petition to the government, 1821

THE UNDERGROUND RAILROAD

The story of the Underground Railroad is filled with daring escapes, secret passwords, disguises and brave heroes. The name makes it sound as if it was a modern subway, but it wasn't a railroad at all, and "Underground" meant "secret." It was a network of trails that runaway slaves could follow from the plantations in the American South to freedom in Canada.

Along these trails, the Underground Railroad offered "stations," or safe houses, where the fugitives could hide from slave hunters. Most important, the Railroad was staffed by "conductors" — women and men, Black and White. These guides defied the law to help fugitives from southern states escape to the 14 free northern states or to Canada.

When Did It Operate?

The Underground Railroad dates from about 1831, the year of Nat Turner's revolt against slavery (see page 15), to 1865, when slavery was abolished in the United States. During that time, slavery was illegal in the northern states, but Black people escaping from southern states often didn't dare to stop there. If they did, they could be caught by slave hunters, who were allowed to recapture slaves and send them back to their masters.

Even worse, in 1850 the Fugitive Slave Act was passed. It declared that anyone in a free northern state who knew about runaway slaves had to turn them in. As a result, the Underground Railroad was most active in the 1850s.

CAUTION!!
COLORED PEOPLE
OF BOSTON, ONE & ALL,
You are hereby respectfully CAUTIONED and advised, to avoid conversing with the
Watchmen and Police Officers
of Boston,
For since the recent ORDER OF THE MAYOR & ALDERMEN, they are empowered to act as
KIDNAPPERS
AND
Slave Catchers,
And they have already been actually employed in KIDNAPPING, CATCHING, AND KEEPING SLAVES. Therefore, if you value your LIBERTY, and the Welfare of the Fugitives among you, Shun them in every possible manner, as so many HOUNDS on the track of the most unfortunate of your race.
Keep a Sharp Look Out for
KIDNAPPERS, and have
TOP EYE open.
APRIL 24, 1851.

Code Words

The people helping runaway slaves had to communicate by mail, and letters could always be opened. So these code words weren't just for fun — they helped confuse slave hunters.

- **Promised land or Canaan:** Canada (in the Bible, Canaan was the promised land to which Moses led the Jews out of slavery in Egypt)
- **Station:** safe house on the route north
- **Freight or cargo:** runaway slaves
- **Station masters or agents:** people who helped hide runaways and direct them to the next station
- **Conductors:** people who acted as guides and travelled with the runaways
- **Stockholders:** people who donated money, food or transportation to runaways

DID YOU KNOW

The name "Underground Railroad" was inspired by the first steam-powered trains in North America. Brand new in the 1830s, trains were a quick and easy way to travel. They were just coming into use when Britain abolished slavery in Canada and all other colonies in 1834.

Runaway slaves couldn't board real trains for fear of getting caught, but they rushed to board the Underground Railroad from that time on.

Josiah Henson's Escape

When Josiah Henson and his family escaped in 1830 from the Kentucky plantation where they lived (see page 13), they took only a small parcel of food and 25 cents. Henson carried the youngest children in a sack on his back. By day, the family hid from the slave catchers. By night, they picked their way through thick woods and swamps. Guided by the North Star, they pressed on for six weeks.

Finally, with the help of the Underground Railroad, the family reached safety and freedom in Upper Canada. When Henson crossed the bridge over the Niagara River, he fell on his knees and kissed the ground.

Passwords and Parcels

The conductors of the Underground Railroad communicated by means of secret passwords and signals — bird calls, special knocks and coded letters like this one:

"Dear Grinnell: Uncle Tom says if the roads are not too bad, you can look for those fleeces of wool by tomorrow. Send them on to test the market and price, no back charges …"

Those "fleeces of wool" were really runaway slaves hiding in a farm cart. Many other tricks were used to transport fugitives. Some enslaved Black people hid in false-bottomed boxes. Others were shipped as freight on real trains. One slave rode across the border stretched out in a coffin — knotholes in the wood gave him just enough air to breathe.

Disguises

Runaway slaves often wore disguises — makeup, wigs and moustaches all helped. Women would dress as men or men as women. Sometimes the runaways dressed up to look like prosperous free Black people living in a northern state — anything to confuse the slave hunters.

The Underground Railroad brought the biggest single group of Black American immigrants to Canada — somewhere between 20 000 and 100 000 people. Nobody knows the exact number because of the secrecy that had to surround the enslaved people's escape.

The Quakers

The Quakers (also called the Society of Friends) were a Christian group in New England who opposed slavery. From the late 1700s on, the Quakers opened their homes to runaway slaves.

As the Underground Railroad grew, the Quakers became station masters and conductors. Levi Coffin was a Quaker and abolitionist who lived in Cincinnati, Ohio. He hid at least 100 enslaved Black people in his home every year and became the "president" of the Underground Railroad. In Canada, Quakers were always eager to help their Black neighbours.

Spirituals

When they were on the plantations, the enslaved Black people had comforted themselves by composing and singing new songs. These "spirituals" — based on Bible stories — expressed their deep longing for their lost homes and their hopes that they would one day be free.

During the Underground Railroad, the words of the songs took on new meanings. One spiritual encouraged reluctant slaves to escape: "Get on board, little children, there's room for many a' more."

Another spiritual told runaways how to find their way to Canada: "Follow the Drinking Gourd." The enslaved people knew these were code words for the Big Dipper constellation. Why was that important? Because the two stars at the front of the Big Dipper's bowl point to the North Star, which guides travellers north.

Underground Railroad Routes

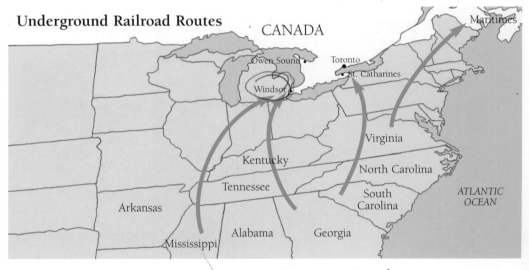

Routes to Freedom

There were several routes that runaway slaves could follow, but they were all dangerous. Men with savage dogs hunted down runaways for rewards. Many runaway slaves were recaptured, cruelly beaten and returned to their plantations.

The escape routes led as directly as possible from slave-holding southern states, such as Tennessee and Mississippi, to free northern states or Canada. Large numbers of Black people crossed the Great Lakes into Upper Canada at towns such as Owen Sound, St. Catharines, Toronto and Windsor. Other routes led to the Maritime provinces.

HARRIET TUBMAN

The most famous conductor on the Underground Railroad was Harriet Tubman. She became known as her people's "Moses," after the biblical leader who led the Jews out of slavery in Egypt.

Born enslaved in 1820, Tubman was forced to do heavy work as a child. A head injury caused by an angry boss gave her narcolepsy for the rest of her life. (Narcolepsy causes a person to fall suddenly into a deep sleep.)

Tubman escaped from the plantation when she was about 30, using skills her father taught her — how to move silently through the forest, how to navigate by the stars, and how to find plants to eat. But she couldn't bear to leave her family in slavery, so she returned and led them all to safety.

More than 300 enslaved Black people were guided to freedom by this dedicated conductor. Dressed as a man, Tubman would approach the slave quarters of a plantation and make her well-known owl-hoot signal. When the slaves heard it, they gathered their belongings and followed her.

Tubman was a strict leader. For the safety of the group, nobody was ever allowed to turn back. As a result, she could say proudly, "I never ran my train off its tracks, and I never lost a passenger."

Until 1858, Harriet Tubman's station on the Underground Railroad was in St. Catharines, Canada West. When the American Civil War broke out in 1861, she returned to the United States to work as a nurse, guide and spy for the northern side. Tubman became the only woman to successfully carry out a rescue during a war — she freed 750 people.

Later, Tubman lived with her parents in Auburn, New York. She died in 1913, and her home is now a museum that honours her courage and extraordinary ability.

Alexander Milton Ross, Conductor

Alexander Milton Ross was a White doctor from Belleville, Canada West, whose hobby was studying birds. Like many other people, he read *Uncle Tom's Cabin*, a novel by Harriet Beecher Stowe that aroused much sympathy for the victims of slavery. Ross decided to do all he could to help enslaved Black people escape.

Using his interest in birds as a cover, Ross made many trips to southern plantations. There, he would befriend the owners while secretly meeting the slaves. Ross gave the slaves clear maps of escape routes or guided them to Canada himself.

The End of the Underground Railroad

In 1865, after the North won the Civil War, slavery came to an end in the United States. Many Black people who had come to Canada on the Underground Railroad returned home. Others remained and became Canadians. But for some years, they lived in fear of being kidnapped by slave hunters who ignored the law.

ISSUE: PREJUDICE AND RACISM

To understand the history of Black Canadians, you must understand prejudice and racism. Black people in Canada have always faced special difficulties because of their race and skin colour.

Prejudice means having an opinion about someone before you have met him or learned much about him. It can also mean having an opinion about a whole race of people, even though you know very little about that race.

Racism is the belief that people's abilities are determined by their race and that one race is better than another. This prejudice can make people treat other races badly. Racist acts — everything from verbal insults to physical violence — are very hurtful to the racial group that is the target.

Prejudice and Racism in Everyday Life

An example of a racial prejudice is "All Black people are good at sports." Of course, it's not a bad thing to be good at sports. But this belief can lead to stereotyping — a prejudiced attitude and oversimplified opinion. When the statement gets repeated often, it can make people forget that Black people are also excellent business people, lawyers, teachers and writers.

An example of a racist act is spray-painting hateful slogans on a Black Canadian church or beating up people of another race just because they're different from you. Extreme racist acts are also called hate crimes.

Why Are Black People Targeted?

Throughout history, Black people have arrived in Canada in waves — Black Loyalists, Jamaican Maroons, refugees from the War of 1812, passengers on the Underground Railroad. Each immigrant group arrived weary from fierce battles or treacherous journeys, but eager to start new lives.

However, Black immigrants often faced prejudice from other Canadian settlers. Darker skin made the newcomers look distinct and, for many of the settlers, was connected with slavery. Also, few former enslaved people could read or write because southern U.S. laws had forbidden their education.

RACISM.
STOP IT!
Raise your hand against racism.

1-888-MARCH21
www.march21.gc.ca

Canada

A History of Prejudice

In the Maritimes, the Black Loyalists (see page 18) struggled to scratch out a living. Along with the Jamaican Maroons (see page 20), many eventually left to look for a better life in Sierra Leone. Later, the refugees from the War of 1812 faced similar problems.

The fugitives who escaped to Upper Canada via the Underground Railroad were also poorly treated by the government and White people in their communities. As a solution, many Black people formed their own communities, with separate schools and churches.

Racism Is Wrong

Prejudice and racism rob all people of something valuable. Young people who experience racism in school or in the community may lose confidence in themselves and their future. They often become angry, which can lead to fighting and other violence.

Nobody can tell by looking at a stranger how that person will behave or what she may achieve. Racist attitudes make it impossible for people to appreciate everyone in their community and share their contributions.

VIOLA DESMOND

On November 8, 1946, Viola Desmond went to a movie at the Roseland Theatre in New Glasgow, Nova Scotia. Despite being a successful businesswoman, she was sold a ticket to the second-rate balcony seats. That's where Black people were expected to sit in those days, not just in Nova Scotia but across Canada.

However, Desmond sat downstairs in the better seats, where only White people were supposed to sit. When she refused to move, the police were called and Desmond was arrested and jailed overnight.

At Desmond's trial, racism wasn't even mentioned. Instead, she was charged with failing to pay a 19-cent extra tax for her downstairs ticket. Desmond was fined $20 and sentenced to 30 days in prison. Fortunately, the Nova Scotia Association for the Advancement of Coloured People, and other friends, helped her win her appeal. Newspapers like the *Clarion* (see Carrie Best, page 49) reported on Desmond's story, and the publicity helped to put an end to this discrimination.

Desmond showed great courage in standing up for her rights. But she was just an ordinary person who represented how many other Black Canadians were feeling about the racism they experienced.

Learning from History

Black history shows that Black Canadians have faced problems just because of their race. More importantly, it reveals the valuable contributions Black people have made in Canada. As people learn more about these contributions, prejudice and racism may diminish. Perhaps then, Black Canadians may fully enjoy their right to live as equals with other Canadians.

DID YOU KNOW

Around the world, legal or formal systems that kept Black and White people apart were called segregation (U.S.A.) or apartheid (South Africa). In Canada, segregation wasn't an official policy. But when Black and White people lived in separate communities, prejudice had a greater chance to spread.

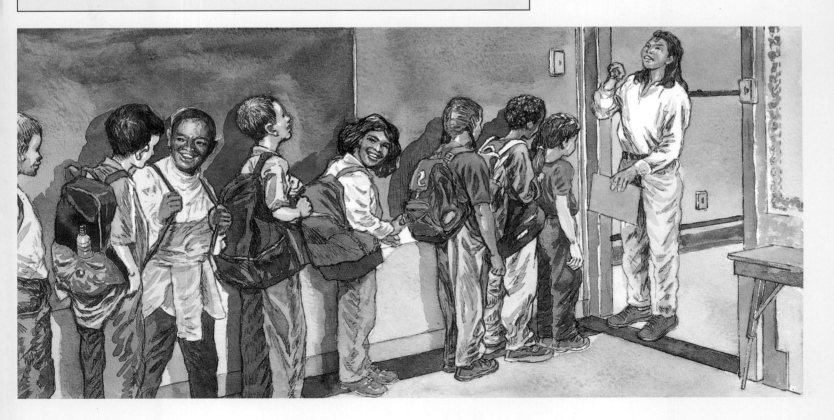

LIFE IN CANADA WEST

By 1850, there were as many as 60 000 free Black people in Canada West (formerly Upper Canada, today Ontario). The recent arrivals needed places to live, as well as jobs to support their families. In the countryside, the Dawn and Elgin Settlements offered schools, work and safe communities.

In Toronto, two enterprising Black men, T.F. Cary and R.B. Richards, opened the city's first ice house. They cut ice from mill ponds in winter and stored it, then sold and delivered it in the summer. Other men found work in hotels or with the new steam railroads. Some women took in laundry or sewing, or became maids in large houses.

The Dawn Settlement

In 1842, Josiah Henson helped establish an all-Black settlement called Dawn near Dresden, Upper Canada. Created by anti-slavery groups, it provided a new beginning for Black American refugees.

The Dawn Settlement boasted a brickyard, a grist mill for grinding grain and a sawmill. Settlers worked at one of these or farmed. The most important building was an industrial training school, one of the first in Canada. Over the next 30 years, the population grew to 500.

Josiah Henson in Canada West

While adjusting to his new found freedom, Josiah Henson helped many other enslaved people to escape. In 1841, he moved with his family to Dresden, then bought land in the Dawn Settlement. Over the years, Henson became Dawn's best-known resident and spokesman.

Henson told stories about his life to writer Harriet Beecher Stowe. He became the inspiration for the Uncle Tom character in Stowe's novel *Uncle Tom's Cabin*, published in 1852. This novel sold 300 000 copies in just its

first year and helped raise awareness about the brutality of slavery. Henson also wrote a book about his own life. He travelled across North America and to England, meeting people and giving speeches.

Josiah Henson 1789-1883   postage/postes

Canada 32

In 1983, Josiah Henson became the first person of African descent to be featured on a Canadian stamp.

"IN REGARD TO CANADA, I LIKE THE COUNTRY ... STILL THERE IS PREJUDICE HERE. THE COLORED PEOPLE ARE TRYING TO REMOVE THIS BY IMPROVING AND EDUCATING THEMSELVES, AND BY INDUSTRY, TO SHOW THAT THEY ARE A PEOPLE WHO HAVE MINDS, AND THAT ALL THEY WANT IS CULTIVATING."

— *Thomas Hedgebeth, Black man who fled North Carolina around 1850*

MARY ANN SHADD

Black teacher and journalist Mary Ann Shadd was born in 1823 in Delaware, a free state. Shadd strongly believed that Black and White people should live together, not in separate communities such as Dawn and Elgin.

When Shadd moved to Canada in 1851, she set up a school for escaped slaves in Windsor, Canada West. She encouraged White children to attend, but many of their parents refused. To change their minds, Shadd started a newspaper called the *Provincial Freeman*, which came out strongly against slavery. Many Americans — Black and White — read Shadd's paper and learned of the Black Canadians' successes.

Shadd closed her school and returned to the United States in 1864 to recruit Black soldiers during the Civil War. Later, she attended law school at Howard University in Washington, D.C. As a lawyer, Shadd fought for many causes, including women's right to vote.

The Buxton Mission School, opened in 1861, set very high standards for its students. Today it's part of the Buxton National Historic Site and Museum, which you can visit to find out more about the Elgin Settlement.

The Elgin Settlement

The Elgin Settlement was the most successful early Black community in Canada West. It was the brainchild of Reverend William King, a White Presbyterian minister.

King opposed slavery, so he was troubled when his father-in-law left him 14 slaves in his will. He decided to start a community near Chatham, Canada West, where he could offer his slaves freedom and a new life. Despite strong protests organized by nearby White people, King founded the Elgin Settlement in 1849.

How Elgin Worked

King felt that ex-slaves needed three things: land, schools and churches. He sold new Black farmers 20 ha (50 acres) of land at a very low price. In return, they had to clear the fields, build houses and dig irrigation ditches.

By 1854, there were 300 families with large livestock herds, grain and tobacco farms, two sawmills and a brick-making company in Elgin. As property owners, Elgin residents even had the right to vote.

Buxton Mission School

Buxton School helped make Elgin successful. With support from the Presbyterian Church, it brought Black and White students together. The curriculum included reading, writing, math, religion, Greek and Latin. Many Buxton graduates became community leaders, doctors, lawyers and teachers.

WEST COAST ADVENTURES

Before the American Civil War, a group of Black Californians were thinking about moving north. Until 1858, they'd been living freely in California. But the new state governor wanted to force African Americans to pay a fee to live in California — and to wear a badge showing they'd paid it. He also allowed a runaway slave to be captured on Californian soil.

Then Black Californians received a message from Vancouver Island, Britain's first colony on the west coast. Governor James Douglas wanted people to come and set up sawmills, mines and salmon fishing operations. He was especially eager to attract educated, hard-working settlers, such as the Black Californians, who would be loyal to Britain.

So Governor Douglas, a fur trader whose mother's ancestors were Black slaves, invited the Black Californians to come and see the new colony.

Governor Douglas Makes a Promise

Governor Douglas made these promises to the Black Californians:

- They could buy land for $5 per 0.4 ha (1 acre).
- They would pay no land taxes for two years.
- After they had owned land for nine months, they could vote and serve as jury members.
- After seven years, they could receive full citizenship rights as British subjects.

The ship the Commodore *brought Black immigrants to Victoria in 1858.*

In return for Governor Douglas's guarantees, the Black Californians were to promise to defend the young colony. Pleased with these arrangements, the Californians encouraged the rest of their community to join them. In April 1858, 400 Black Californian families sailed from San Francisco to Victoria, the colony's most important town. Vancouver Island remained a welcoming place for Black people until Governor Douglas retired in 1864.

Gold Rush

In 1858, gold was discovered in the Fraser River on the British Columbia mainland. By year's end, 20 000 prospectors had passed through Victoria in search of gold. Governor Douglas was worried that these gold seekers, most of them Americans, might try to claim the territory for the United States. Just in case, he enforced stern justice in the wild new mining towns. He knew that, if necessary, he could count on the loyal support of the Black Californians.

"I WAS ONE OF THE SUCCESSFUL GOLD PROSPECTORS IN BRITISH COLUMBIA, ALTHOUGH THERE WERE 10 YEARS OF DOUBT WHEN I NEVER MADE A SINGLE STRIKE! ... I WAS NOT ONE TO GIVE UP AND I'M GLAD I KEPT TRYING ... IN 1884 WE FOUND SEVERAL GOLD-BEARING STREAMS AROUND LORNE CREEK. I UNDERSTAND THAT ONE OF THE STREAMS WAS LATER CALLED MCDAME."

— *Henry McDame, Black prospector*

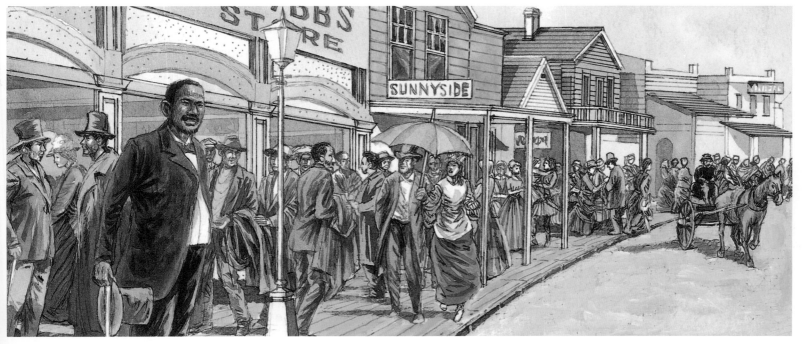

Life on Vancouver Island

The Black Californians were determined to succeed on Vancouver Island. Most stayed in Victoria and opened new businesses. The finest restaurant in Victoria, Ringo's, and the best barbershop were both owned by Black businessmen.

John Sullivan Deas was another successful Black entrepreneur. Trained as a tinsmith, he took over a salmon canning factory on the Fraser River and shipped thousands of cases of salmon to Britain every year. Other Black people couldn't resist adventure in the gold rush.

Mifflin Gibbs

The first Black politician in Canada, Mifflin Gibbs, was elected to Victoria City Council in 1867. A good businessman, Gibbs ran a general store that competed with the Hudson's Bay Company and also built a coal mine and a railway in the Queen Charlotte Islands. In 1868, Gibbs was a delegate at the convention that decided that British Columbia would become part of Canada.

SYLVIA STARK

Sylvia Stark was one of British Columbia's first pioneers. Born a slave in Missouri in 1839, she learned to read by watching White children do their lessons. When she was ten, her father bought freedom for the family, and in 1851 they moved to California.

Sylvia married Louis Stark and had two children. When California introduced restrictions against Black people, the family fled north, arriving on Saltspring Island (near Vancouver Island) in 1860. Their 15 dairy cows were lowered into the water by ropes so they could swim ashore.

While Louis ran the farm, Sylvia had two more children and became a volunteer midwife and nurse. Years later, the Starks survived a smallpox epidemic, then moved to the Nanaimo area. But Sylvia missed Saltspring. She returned to the island, where she died at age 106.

In 1860, the Black Californians formed the Victoria Pioneer Rifle Company to guard Vancouver Island against any American attack.

BACK TO THE U.S.

During the 1850s — thanks to the Underground Railroad — about 60 000 Black people were living in Canadian provinces. In towns and on farms, newly free Black people were making decent lives for themselves. By contrast, their American cousins in the southern states were still enslaved.

The Black Canadian community was full of hope. But they had some worries, including how to get a good education for their children.

Black parents believed strongly that their children deserved good schools. But many schools in Canada didn't want Black students, or forced them to sit at the back of the classroom. After the American Civil War, this problem became an important reason why many Black people returned to the United States.

Segregated vs. Integrated Schools

In 1850, the Common Schools Act was passed in Canada West. This law allowed separate schools for Black and White children. A few years later, a similar law was passed in Nova Scotia. All-Black schools were built, but they had little money. Often the buildings were second-rate and the teachers poorly paid.

Many Black students failed to learn in these segregated schools. Integrated schools such as Buxton School and Mary Ann Shadd's school, where Black and White children studied together, worked better. Toronto also had integrated schools. Many Black graduates from these schools went on to university and had successful careers.

Civil War!

Black Canadians were distracted from their problems when the Civil War broke out in the United States in 1861. The abolition of slavery was a major goal of many of those fighting on the side of the anti-slavery states of the north against the pro-slavery states of the south. At first, Black Americans weren't allowed to fight. But Frederick Douglass, a famous Black abolitionist, got that changed.

Black Canadians wanted to fight against slavery, too. Josiah Henson, Mary Ann Shadd and Harriet Tubman returned to the United States to recruit Black soldiers. Thousands of Black Canadians joined the Union army of the northern states, and many died.

After the Civil War

The Civil War ended with the northern side winning. Across the American South, homes, schools, farms and train tracks were destroyed. Newly freed slaves — 14 million of them — needed schooling and work. During a period called the Reconstruction, the American government tried to rebuild and find ways for Black and White people to live together in a non-slave society.

The Reconstruction Act of 1867 stated that "all persons born in the United States are citizens and have equal rights, and that all male citizens have the right to vote, regardless of race, color, or having been a slave."

An organization called the Freedmen's Bureau set up hospitals and public schools for Black people across the southern states. In addition, African Americans were given the right to buy land and enter politics.

The News Reaches Canada

After the Civil War, Canadian newspapers reported that slavery had ended in the United States.

When Black Canadians learned that many improvements were being made to benefit former slaves, it made them think. Should they stay in Canada or go back to the United States? They also learned that well-funded public schools were being set up in the South and began to feel that their children might have better lives there.

Goodbye, Canada

The pull to return to the United States was strong. In Canada, Black people were having a hard time finding good jobs. Many wanted to reunite with family and friends back home. White Canadians did little to stop them from leaving. Some felt that Black people should return home, and others wanted to stop any more Black refugees from coming to Canada.

For one reason or another, over the next 30 years about two-thirds of the Black people in Canada returned to the United States, hoping for a better life. Canada's Black population declined from 60 000 to 18 000.

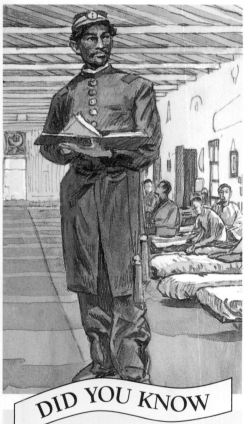

DID YOU KNOW

In 1857, Dr. Anderson Ruffin Abbott became the first Black graduate of Toronto's Medical College. He served as a surgeon for the Union army during the Civil War, then returned to Canada.

COWBOYS AND PIONEERS

In 1867, the Dominion of Canada was created when Canada East (Quebec), Canada West (Ontario), New Brunswick and Nova Scotia joined together. The Canadian government quickly realized that the country would be much stronger if it was bigger. But how should it expand?

The government soon began to look west. It saw buffalo herds still roaming on endless grassland stretching west to the mountains. The Cree and other Native peoples were living on the land and hunting for game. But the government wanted pioneers to settle down and farm the land instead. It also planned to push the Canadian Pacific Railway all the way west. Only then could Canada expand from coast to coast.

"The Last Best West"
In the 1890s, Canada began to advertise cheap land in the Prairies to attract settlers from Europe and the United States. Among those tempted to take up this offer were African Americans living in the midwestern states.

To Black people who weren't firmly settled by 1905, Canadian railway and government posters looked very attractive. They had headlines such as "The Last Best West," and they advertised land at $2 per 0.4 ha (1 acre) in Saskatchewan — the price in the neighbouring state of North Dakota was $50.

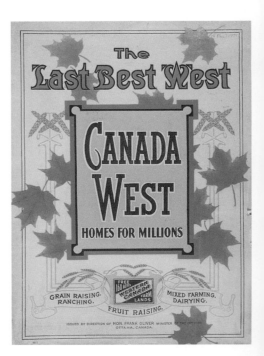

PROFILE

JOHN WARE

John Ware was born enslaved in the United States, but he was freed at the end of the Civil War. He became a cowboy in Texas, then moved to Alberta in 1882.

Tall and powerful, Ware knew all about handling horses and throwing a lasso. He became a famous rodeo cowboy who could wrestle a steer to the ground. One story tells how he rode over a cliff into a river while trying to tame a bucking horse. The spectators were amazed when Ware and the horse came up alive, with Ware still in the saddle!

John Ware married Mildred Lewis after he came to Canada, and together they raised five children and ran a successful ranch. Ware died in 1905, when his horse stumbled in a hole, fell and crushed him. Today you can visit the John Ware Historic Cabin in Dinosaur Provincial Park near Calgary, Alberta.

Black Pioneers
Between 1905 and 1909, many hundreds of Black Americans journeyed north from their homes to the Canadian Prairies. Most travelled by train and arrived at small border towns in Manitoba and Saskatchewan. Some of the immigrants chose to make their homes in those provinces.

But the majority of Black Americans journeyed west to Alberta. Some went to booming cities such as Edmonton. Others decided to live in rural areas as cowboys or homesteaders.

Homesteading

When the Black pioneers arrived in the Prairies, they found land covered with trees and underbrush. It took weeks to clear the land, especially because they often had to work without horses or oxen. A pioneer's first house was usually a log cabin with a sod (grass and earth) roof. Neighbours — whether Black or White — helped one another build their homes. The pioneers planted large gardens and hunted for fresh meat such as deer, duck, pheasant and rabbit.

Working in Winter Weather

Some Black homesteaders took on extra work during the winter. They hauled heavy loads by sleigh to northern settlements such as Fort McMurray, Alberta, where the railroad didn't reach.

There were no inns where the men could sleep. To keep warm at night, they'd scoop out snow from a snowbank, lay down spruce boughs to make a sleeping mat, then pile more snow over their blankets.

A few years later, when the Canadian government wanted to restrict Black immigration, it made ridiculous claims, including that Black people weren't suited to Canada's cold climate. Brave Black homesteaders had already proved how wrong that was!

Surviving in a Cold Climate

How did Black settlers from southern climates manage to survive in the frozen north? Take a look at life in a small community north of Edmonton, Alberta. In the early 1900s, Amber Valley was the largest rural Black settlement in western Canada.

One of its first settlers, Martha Edwards, lived with her husband, Jeff, in her father's log cabin. There was no bathtub or toilet. The wind howled through cracks in the walls. But Martha says they made do by stuffing the cracks with rags and loading up on warm bedding and firewood. For Christmas, the family ate prairie chicken (grouse) and moose meat, instead of turkey.

These Black settlers learned how to survive in Canada's cold climate very well. The children, grandchildren and great-grandchildren of hardy pioneer families such as the Edwards still live in the Amber Valley area.

THE EXODUSTERS

By the 1880s, the promise of a good life for freed slaves in the United States was over. In the South, violent anti-Black groups such as the Ku Klux Klan had formed, and new laws forced the segregation of Black and White people.

Fifty thousand Black Americans escaped by heading west to new states such as Oklahoma.

Most were poor farm labourers — known as Exodusters — who went to take up offers of free land. Many Exodusters did well in Oklahoma, creating large cattle ranches. But some farmers were hit by drought and floods, and others found that land was becoming too expensive. They began to think about moving north to Canada.

Trouble in Oklahoma

By 1910, things were getting worse for the Exodusters in Oklahoma. The state had passed segregation laws like the ones in the southern states. More and more Black families looked towards Canada as a refuge from prejudice and violence.

A group of Black people travelled to the Canadian Prairies to investigate. One of them was Henry Sneed, a former Texan, who liked what he saw. When he returned to Oklahoma, Sneed helped to organize a large group of Exodusters who had decided to emigrate to Canada. Knowing Canada's record, they were sure they would be welcomed.

Protests from White Canadians

Up until 1911, under Prime Minister Sir Wilfrid Laurier, Canada had actively recruited Black settlers to the Prairies. Now, anti-Black prejudice was starting to build. Newspapers ran stories about problems that sprang up when large numbers of Black people moved to northern American cities. But the papers didn't report on Black people's success stories.

When White Canadians heard rumours that a large group of Exodusters was planning to come north, many called for an end to Black immigration.

Discouragement from Canada

Faced with protests from White Canadians, Prime Minister Laurier decided he had to discourage the Exodusters from coming to Canada.

One government scheme sent Dr. G.W. Miller, a Black doctor from Chicago, to hold meetings in Oklahoma, Kansas and other western states. In his speeches, Dr. Miller tried to convince hopeful farmers that they would perish in Canada's waist-high snows. The ground was frozen year-round, he said, so they wouldn't be able to farm it.

The government also instructed officials at the border to make Black Americans answer tough questions about their health and character. The idea was that they would fail the test and be sent back home.

Canada, Here We Come!

The Exodusters had faced discouragement before and won. Encouraged by Henry Sneed's report on Canada, a group of about 190 Black people from Oklahoma and Kansas made the trek north in 1911. They filled nine railway cars with horses and farming tools.

At the Canadian border, officials tried to stump the Exodusters with health and citizenship tests. But because the group had money, property and good health, they passed easily. They went on to establish communities from western Alberta to Thunder Bay, Ontario. Between 1909 and 1911, about 1500 Exodusters emigrated from Oklahoma to the Canadian Prairies.

CANADA WILL BAR THE NEGRO OUT

Official Notice Given by Dominion to United States Consul

UNFITTED FOR HEALTHY CLIMATE

The Action of Dominion Leading to Conference in Washington

Washington, D.C. April 26. — The plans of the Dominion of Canada to adopt restrictions against the entering of their country by American negroes was the subject of a conference today between Assistant Secretary of State Wilson and John K. Jones, consul general of the U.S. at Winnipeg. Mr. Jones presented a recommendation from the Canadian immigration authorities indicating that the American negro may be barred on the ground that he could not become adapted to the rigorous northern climate and consequently might become a public charge. Such action is authorized by the immigration act of Canada.

The name "Exodusters" comes from the book of Exodus in the Bible, which tells the story of the Israelites' flight from slavery in Egypt. "Exodus" means the departure of a large group of people, and "dusters" refers to the dry soil of Oklahoma.

◆ PROFILE ◆

MATTIE MAYES

Mattie Mayes was a successful Oklahoman immigrant. In 1910, when she was 60 years old, she and her husband, Joe, travelled by train to Canada with 13 children and grandchildren and 10 other families.

The group chose to homestead in Eldon, not far from North Battleford, Saskatchewan. After 10 years of their hard work, Mattie's farm was doing well. The community built a Baptist church, and Joe became the first preacher. A few years later, they built a school.

Mattie was a warm and caring leader in the community until she died in 1953 at age 103. Her descendents include Reuben Mayes, the great NFL football player, and Lesa Stringer, who's been a member of Canada's national women's bobsleigh team.

Stopping Black Immigration

Still worried by western protests, Laurier's government decided to stop Black immigration for one year — from 1911 to 1912. It passed a regulation stating that Black people were "unsuitable to the climate and requirements of Canada."

Although the regulation never became law, Black people got the message that they were no longer welcome in Canada. In fact, Black immigration to Canada came to a standstill from 1912 until the 1950s.

FIGHTING IN TWO WORLD WARS

In the 20th century, Canada fought in two world wars. Twice, Canadian soldiers, sailors and fliers went overseas to help defend Britain and its Allies. Black Canadians wanted to show their loyalty to Britain and also help Canada — still a young country — come together as a nation.

Black Canadians also knew that, in order to be treated equally with White Canadians, they needed to accept the dangers of war. But serving their country proved to be difficult.

World War I

On August 4, 1914, Germany, under its leader, Kaiser Wilhelm II, invaded Belgium. That same day, Britain declared war on Germany and its empire. All the countries of the British Empire, including Canada, sent troops to fight on the battlefields of France.

Black Canadians lined up at recruitment offices to volunteer for service. But thousands were turned away. Some White officers said that Black and White soldiers shouldn't mix. Black Canadian leaders, newspaper reporters and clergymen protested strongly, and by 1915 a few Black soldiers were allowed to join White regiments.

Nova Scotia No. 2 Construction Battalion

In 1916, an all-Black unit of 600 men called the No. 2 Construction Battalion was formed. They weren't allowed to fight, but they cut lumber in France, built huts for soldiers at the battlefronts and dug trenches.

Training took place in both Pictou and Truro, Nova Scotia, where the battalion formed its own brass band to lead marches. In 1917, the men sailed across the Atlantic Ocean, always under threat from enemy submarines. Among the soldiers were the sons of cowboy John Ware (see page 36). After the war, No. 2 Battalion was praised for its discipline and faithful service.

It took almost two years of protesting and lobbying by Black Canadians before the No. 2 Construction Battalion was formed. Its first headquarters, in Pictou, Nova Scotia, is now a National Historic Site.

On the Home Front

Black Canadians formed patriotic clubs that raised money to support the war effort. Men volunteered to work on farms and in factories and hospitals. In Vancouver, women formed a branch of the Universal Black Cross nurses to care for wounded Black servicemen.

Between the Wars

World War I was a time of pride and sorrow for Black Canadians. They were proud of their war efforts, but by the time the war ended in 1918, many Black soldiers were wounded or dead. Black Canadians hoped that their wartime service would lead to better relations between the races at home.

In 1919, Black American Marcus Garvey, who was born in Jamaica, opened branches of his Universal Negro Improvement Association (now the Universal African Improvement Association) in Canada. Its goal was to help Black people develop a sense of pride by gaining better jobs and working for their rights. The organization also encouraged Black people to return to Africa.

Black Canadians were becoming more aware of their heritage. In the 1920s, Montreal, with its many jazz clubs, became a lively centre of Black culture. Black Canadians were full of hope for their future.

But in the 1930s, the Depression brought poverty and hard times across Canada. However, it also helped improve race relations by bringing people together. No matter what their skin colour, most people were desperately poor and needed to help one another to survive.

World War II

World War II broke out in 1939. Germany, led by Adolf Hitler and the Nazi Party, invaded Czechoslovakia and Poland. Britain, Canada and the Allies declared war, vowing to stop Hitler.

In this war, Black Canadians had an easier time enlisting in the army, navy and air force, but there were still difficulties. They refused to serve in

"DO NOT LET ANY MAN TELL YOU DIFFERENT, NO MAN IS ANY BRAVER THAN A BLACK MAN. ... AFTER ALL, THE BLACK MAN WENT OVER THERE, HE TRAINED LIKE A SOLDIER, HE FOUGHT LIKE A SOLDIER AND HE DIED LIKE A SOLDIER, AND THAT IS ALL ANY WHITE MAN CAN DO."

— *Sergeant A. Seymour Tyler, Black Canadian World War II veteran*

segregated units like the Construction Battalion. Instead, they fought in racially mixed units and helped Britain and its Allies win the war in 1945.

After the Wars

Black Canadians' participation in two world wars led to better race relations. White Canadians realized that Black sons and daughters — just like their own children — had given their lives for their country. As well, returning Black soldiers would not tolerate the discrimination of the past. It was time to ensure that all races were treated equally in Canada.

During World War II, Black women were allowed to work in weapons factories. For most of them, it was their first chance to escape from domestic work such as child-minding and housekeeping.

• PROFILE •

THE CARTY BROTHERS

The Carty family of Saint John, New Brunswick, sent seven sons to World War II. Adolphus, William, Clyde, Donald and Gerald Carty all enlisted in the air force, while Robert and Malcolm joined the army. The brothers fought hard for their country and at the close of the war, all seven were discharged with high rank.

WORKING FOR RESPECT

Before World War II, Black Canadian men and women were kept out of many jobs and professions. They couldn't attend nursing schools or teachers' colleges, join hockey leagues or belong to trade unions. Only the lowest-paying jobs were open to them.

In cities such as Halifax and Toronto, 80 per cent of Black women worked as domestic servants in White Canadian homes. Many men worked for the railway as porters. But these were all dead-end jobs because they didn't allow for promotion to better positions.

Work as a Railway Porter
Starting in the early 1900s, large numbers of Black men were hired as railway porters. Porters carried suitcases for passengers, shined shoes and made up beds in the overnight sleeping cars.

Being a porter was one of the few steady jobs Black men could get at that time. So they came to Montreal (where the hiring was done) from across Canada, the United States and the Caribbean islands, wanting to work for Canadian Pacific Railway and Canadian National Railways.

Porters' wages were low, but the men could earn good tips. Still, they had to endure racist remarks from some White passengers, and they were separated from their families for days and weeks at a time.

Work as a Domestic Servant
Domestic servants spent the day cleaning their employer's house, caring for the children and sometimes cooking meals. These Black women were lucky if their employer was fair and kind. Then in the evening, the women had to go home and do the same work for their own families.

The pay was poor and, because they worked alone, it was hard for the women to band together and demand better conditions. Most women were paid less than men, even for the same work.

A Sense of Community

Travelling from coast to coast, porters kept in touch with Black people across the country. In Winnipeg, the men got together at Haynes Chicken Shack. This famous restaurant was owned by Piercy Haynes, a railway worker, boxer and jazz pianist.

While their husbands were away working on the railways, some Black women in Toronto formed the Eureka Friendly Club. They met every other Thursday afternoon to share a meal and listen to music. A favourite song was "Some of These Days," written by the African Canadian Shelton Brooks.

Ray Lewis of Hamilton, Ontario, was the first porter who was also a world-class athlete. Lewis not only trained hard, but he had to overcome racial insults while working on the railway. In 1932, Lewis brought home a bronze medal as part of the 4 x 400 relay team at the Los Angeles Olympics. In 2001, Lewis received the Order of Canada, the highest honour awarded to a person by the Government of Canada.

The Brotherhood of Sleeping Car Porters

In 1919, Black porters formed a union — an organization to help them fight for better jobs. It was the first Canadian union to allow Black members. But for years the union had little success.

After World War II, the president of the American Brotherhood of Sleeping Car Porters, A. Philip Randolph, helped the porters set up branches of his union in Canada. By 1955, the new union — the Canadian Brotherhood of Sleeping Car Porters — had won its struggle. From then on, a Black porter could be promoted to dining-car waiter or conductor.

Hard-Won Respect

In 1944, Ontario became the first province to pass an act to prevent discrimination against any person because of race or religion. Other provinces soon followed.

When Black Canadian men were fighting in World War II, women took over their jobs in factories and other workplaces. Many Black women liked these jobs better than domestic service. But when the men came home to Canada, they wanted their jobs back. Some Black women returned to domestic service, but many upgraded their education, found new job opportunities and fought for racial equality and women's rights.

Railway porters continued to improve their working conditions. Through their efforts, the porters created new and better opportunities for Black people in Canada.

PROFILE

STANLEY G. GRIZZLE

Born in Toronto in 1918, Stanley G. Grizzle was a railway porter who became president of the Toronto branch of the Brotherhood of Sleeping Car Porters. He spent the 1950s campaigning for equal rights for Black people.

Grizzle was the first Black judge in Ontario's Citizenship Court and the first African Canadian to run for election to the Ontario legislature. In recognition of his distinguished service, he received the Order of Canada in 1995.

CARIBBEAN AND AFRICAN IMMIGRANTS

Canada is often called a country of immigrants. But Canada hasn't always welcomed everybody who wants to be an immigrant.

During the first half of the 20th century, Canada encouraged White people from Europe and the United States to come. They were known as the "preferred nationalities." Very few Black people were able to immigrate.

But after World War II, Canadian immigration policy began to change, thanks in large part to Black activists such as Harry Gairey and Donald Moore. They helped open the door for Black immigrants from the Caribbean, Guyana (South America) and Africa.

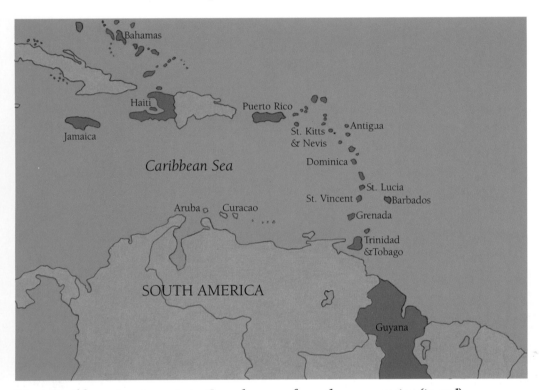

Most Caribbean immigrants to Canada come from these countries (in red).

Blue Skies, Tropical Seas

The Caribbean, also called the West Indies, is a chain of island countries including Barbados, Jamaica, St. Lucia and Trinidad. The tropical climate brings hot sunshine, rainy seasons and hurricanes.

Most Caribbean people are of African descent. For centuries, European countries operated sugar plantations in the Caribbean using slave labour. By the 1960s, most of these countries had gained their independence. But many people remained poor or had trouble finding jobs.

Black Canadian Activists

In 1954, a group of 35 Black Canadian activists met with federal Cabinet ministers (government leaders) in Ottawa. The group wanted to change the Immigration Act of 1952 because it discriminated against people of colour. One of the group's leaders, Donald Moore, reminded the Cabinet ministers of Black Canadians' heroic service in the world wars.

After years of pressure, the government passed a new Immigration Act in 1962. Would-be immigrants could no longer be discriminated against because of their race or religion.

The West Indian Domestic Scheme

In 1955, the government took a first step in opening up Black immigration. The Domestic Scheme encouraged Caribbean women to come to Canada, but only if they promised to work as domestic servants for one year. Many women took the opportunity — 2700 over the next 10 years. Often they left behind husbands and children.

After their year of domestic service, many women enrolled in university or worked as teachers, nurses and office workers. Later, they brought their families to Canada.

The Points System

Canada still needed a better way than the Immigration Act of 1962 and the Domestic Scheme to decide who would be allowed to immigrate. In 1967, a method called the points system was introduced. People who wished to immigrate were awarded points for such things as education, job skills and ability to speak English or French. Anyone who obtained at least 70 points out of 100 was allowed to immigrate. Now hopeful immigrants from all countries had a fair chance.

Adjusting to Canada

Some Caribbean immigrants had problems adjusting to Canada. The winters felt bitterly cold. Fathers or mothers who came on their own were lonely until they could bring their families. They had to get used to new customs and different ways of

Quick Facts

Waves of Black Immigration to Canada

1783	Black Loyalists
1796	Jamaican Maroons
1814	Refugees of the War of 1812
1831–1865	Underground Railroad
1858	Black Californians
1911	Oklahoma Exodusters
1955	Caribbean Domestic Service Workers
1967	Caribbean Immigrants, from the Caribbean and from England
1980	African Immigrants

• PROFILE •

CARIBBEAN IMMIGRANTS

Under the points system, many Caribbean people were well qualified to immigrate. During the 1970s and 1980s, 315 000 immigrated to Canada, mostly from Jamaica, Trinidad and Haiti.

Black people from the Caribbean, unlike earlier Black immigrants, settled mainly in the cities. English-speaking people found jobs in Toronto or other cities across the country where English was the main language. French-speaking Haitians moved to Montreal. Canada has been enriched by the skills and the culture that Caribbean immigrants brought with them.

speaking. Even the many people from the Caribbean who had immigrated first to Britain and then to Canada found the adjustment difficult.

Black people were the majority in the Caribbean, but in Canada they stood out in the sea of White faces. Their children had to adjust to a different school system. And the new immigrants didn't always feel welcomed by their White Canadian neighbours.

Community Support

Black Canadians already settled here were eager to help the Caribbean newcomers. They worked together to offer young people dance, drama and music programs, as well as, academic scholarships, especially in Ontario. Carnivals, concerts and picnics were some of the traditions they continued.

Like other Black Canadians, Caribbean immigrants entered politics, started businesses and wrote books. They became involved in already-established magazines and newspapers, such as *Contrast*, for the

community. Today, most of Canada's Black population is of Caribbean background.

Black African Immigrants

Since 1980, immigrants have come to Canada directly from Africa. They hail from many different countries, including Ghana, Nigeria, Senegal, Sierra Leone, Somalia and South Africa. Some are refugees from famine and war and include doctors, musicians, business owners and writers.

CELEBRATING BLACK HERITAGE

In December 1995, February was declared Black History Month across Canada, thanks to the work of the Ontario Black History Society (OBHS). During this time, the OBHS focuses media attention on Black Canadian history and helps schools, libraries and community groups promote Black Canadian heritage.

There are many other associations that keep Black Canadian heritage alive, including the PRUDE Community Access Centre, with its motto of "Pride, Race, Unity, Dignity, Education." The Black Cultural Centre in Dartmouth, Nova Scotia, the first of its kind in Canada, educates people about Black people's roots, heritage and identity.

Black Canadian History Tours
In southwestern Ontario, the African Canadian Heritage Tour brings Black history to life. Visitors can tour museums and churches and see special exhibitions from the days of the Underground Railroad. A trail through the woods — complete with scary sound effects — gives a sense of the dangers the slaves faced when escaping to freedom in Canada.

Special bus tours in Niagara Falls and Toronto also tell about Black history in these cities.

Heritage Festivals

• **Emancipation Day:** Slavery officially ended in all British territories, including Canada, on July 31, 1833. Since 1834, many Black people around the world have celebrated August 1 as Emancipation Day.

• **Kwanzaa:** This week-long celebration began in 1966. It was inspired by African harvest festivals — Kwanzaa means "first fruits" in the Swahili language. The festivities run from December 26 to New Year's Day. Many Black Canadians gather with friends and family to remember their history and enjoy special feasts. They light seven candles, each one representing a high ideal to guide people in their lives: unity, self-determination, responsibility, co-operation, purpose, creativity and faith.

• **Caribana:** In the Caribbean islands, people celebrate Carnival in February, just before the Christian season of Lent. In 1967, when Canada turned 100 years old, Black Canadians in Toronto decided to organize their own Centennial event. They called it Caribana and shifted it to August to help celebrate Emancipation Day and a long weekend in summer.

Caribana (now called the Toronto International Carnival) has become a huge annual summer party. Groups prepare all year for the parade, with its steel-drum music, fantastic costumes and non-stop dancing. More than 1 million people attend Caribana from all over North America. Similar celebrations take place in Halifax, Montreal, Windsor and other cities across Canada.

PROFILE

AFRICVILLE

Africville was a Black community on the north side of Halifax. Although its story is sad, many Black Canadians feel it should be remembered.

Starting in 1848, Africville attracted Black people from across Nova Scotia who were looking for jobs in Halifax. The town grew to 400 residents by 1951. It was a tight-knit community with the Baptist church at its centre. Some Africville residents worked on trading ships, while others helped to construct Halifax buildings. Some people started their own businesses and owned houses and land.

But problems began almost immediately. In the 1850s, a railway cut through the community. Although the residents paid taxes to Halifax, the city never provided water, sewage or police services. Instead, it located factories, a prison and a garbage dump beside the community. To any outsider, Africville looked like a slum.

In the 1960s, without consulting the residents, Halifax's city council decided to get rid of Africville. Black community leaders protested loudly, saying the residents didn't want to leave. Instead, they needed and deserved the services they'd been denied. However, Africville's houses were destroyed and the people were moved. They were promised better homes, but their new houses were often worse.

The spirit of Africville lives on in the memory of Black Nova Scotians. Every year people gather in the parkland where the town once stood to remember a special community. In 2002, Africville was declared a National Historic Site in recognition of its importance to Black Canadian culture.

Religious Heritage

Religion is another way of preserving one's heritage. Black Canadians today practise a variety of religions. Some are Roman Catholics, others attend Protestant churches, including the British Methodist Episcopal Church of Canada and the African United Baptist Association. Martin Luther King Jr., a leader of the civil rights movement in the United States in the 1960s, was a Baptist minister.

Other Black Canadians are Muslims, followers of Islam. Some Canadians were inspired by Malcolm X, an American Muslim leader in the civil rights movement. Many recent African immigrants are also Muslims.

Some Black Canadians are Rastafarians. This faith group began in Jamaica in the 1930s. Rastafarians celebrate their African heritage, believing that the last Ethiopian emperor — Haile Selassie — was divine.

Black History on the Screen and Stage

Black Canadians also explore their heritage through movies and theatre. Filmmakers have uncovered almost-forgotten stories from Black history. Montreal's Black Theatre Workshop and Toronto's Obsidian Theatre Company perform plays with Black Canadian themes, train young actors and tour schools.

YESTERDAY, TODAY AND TOMORROW

Canada's Black population boasts many skilled and talented people who have achieved fame in a variety of fields. Some have overcome significant challenges in order to make important contributions to Canada.

Many young Black people are coming forward to help shape Canada's future. They still have to fight racism and prejudice, but if they have the strength and courage to keep trying, they will make Canada a better country.

Here are just a few of the many well-known Black Canadians.

MUSICIANS

Deborah Cox was born in Toronto in 1974. Inspired by Black singers such as Gladys Knight and Bob Marley, Cox became Canada's first Black female rhythm and blues diva. In 1992, she performed at the inauguration of the new U.S. president, Bill Clinton. Cox is a volunteer with World Vision Canada, a non-profit organization that sponsors poor children around the world.

Soprano **Measha Brueggergosman** was only 20 years old in 1998 when she starred in a new Canadian opera called *Beatrice Chancy*. Born in Fredericton, New Brunswick, Brueggergosman is on her way to a brilliant international career. She often ends her concerts by singing Black spirituals that celebrate her roots.

World-famous jazz pianist **Oscar Peterson** was born in Montreal in 1925. At 14, he won a national contest for amateur musicians. Peterson was still in his twenties when he dazzled the audience with his flying fingers at New York's famous Carnegie Hall. A composer as well as a jazz pianist, Peterson has won many awards and is a Companion of the Order of Canada.

The first really successful Canadian rap artist was **Maestro Fresh Wes**. He was born in Toronto in 1968 to Guyanese parents. His first album sold more than 150 000 copies in Canada, and on his second album, he rapped about the Black Canadian identity. The Maestro won the first Canadian Juno Award for "Best Rap Recording" in 1991.

POLITICIANS

Elected as a federal Progressive Conservative in 1968, **Lincoln Alexander** was appointed Minister of Labour in 1979, becoming the first Black Canadian to serve in Cabinet. In 1985, at the age of 63, he was appointed Lieutenant-Governor of Ontario — another first for a Black Canadian.

Born in Jamaica in 1930, **Rosemary Brown** came to Canada as a student. She enjoyed debating at university and soon found herself involved in politics, becoming the first Black Canadian woman elected to the British Columbia legislature. Brown served as a member of the New Democratic Party until 1986. Since then, she has taught at Simon Fraser University in British Columbia, and been appointed Chief Commissioner of the Ontario Human Rights Commission.

Daurene Lewis is a seventh-generation Nova Scotian from Annapolis Royal. (One of her ancestors, Rose Fortune, became Canada's first policewoman around 1783.) Lewis graduated from Dalhousie University in Halifax, and later taught nursing. From 1984 to 1988, she was the mayor of Annapolis Royal, the first Black woman mayor in North America.

WRITERS AND STORYTELLERS

Carrie Best of New Glasgow, Nova Scotia, was the publisher of a newspaper called the *Clarion* in the 1940s and 1950s. Best was a fearless journalist who demanded fair treatment for Black people. By making sure that Black Canadians were served in restaurants and admitted to theatres, Best helped make Canada a better place to live. She received the Order of Canada in recognition of her fight for her community.

"I AM A PERSON, BORN IN THE IMAGE OF GOD. I HAVE INTELLIGENCE, I AM HONEST, AND I AM AS GOOD, IF NOT BETTER THAN ANYBODY WHO WALKS THE FACE OF THIS EARTH …"

— *Carrie Best*

Trinidad-born **Dionne Brand** came to Toronto, Ontario, in 1970 when she was just 17 years old. Now she's a well-known writer, filmmaker and human rights activist. Brand's many books include *Land to Light On*, which won a Governor General's Award in 1997, and *Earth Magic*, a poetry collection for children.

Born in Nova Scotia in 1960, **George Elliott Clarke** has received many awards for his poetry, and is also known as a playwright and screenwriter. In 1997, Clarke wrote the libretto (words) for James Rolfe's opera, *Beatrice Chancy*. The story takes place in Nova Scotia's Annapolis Valley in 1801, when slavery was still a way of life. The opera's first performances starred Measha Brueggergosman (see page 48).

The Caribbean tradition of storytelling followed **Rita Cox** from Trinidad to Canada. When Cox tells her ghost stories, fables and animal stories, children gather round. This storyteller also founded the Black Heritage and West Indies Collection, one of the most important collections of writings about and by Black people. Cox received the Governor General's 1992 Commemorative Medal for her contributions to Canada.

Children's author **Tololwa M. Mollel** was born in Tanzania, Africa, in 1952. Since moving to Edmonton, Alberta, Mollel has published more than 15 books — including *The Orphan Boy* and *Kitoto the Mighty* — and has won many awards. He runs storytelling and drama workshops for children around North America.

ATHLETES

Called "the world's fastest human," **Donovan Bailey** has been clocked running at a speed of 43.6 km/h (27 m.p.h.). Born in 1967 in Jamaica, Bailey grew up in Oakville, Ontario. As a sprinter, Bailey won a gold medal in the 100 metre race at the 1996 Olympics in Atlanta, setting a world record of 9.84 seconds. He was also a member of the Canadian 4 x 100 relay team that won gold at the same Olympic Games.

DID YOU KNOW

Donovan Bailey is one of the few athletes to be an Olympic gold medallist, World Champion and world record holder. In 1996 he was also named Canada's Athlete of the Year.

In 1990, **Charmaine Crooks** of North Vancouver became the first Canadian woman to run 800 metres in less than 2 minutes. Born in Jamaica, the sprinter made the Canadian Olympic team in 1980, when she was only 16. Crooks has since competed in a record five Olympic Games. Today, she's a television host and public speaker.

During the final men's hockey game of the 2002 Olympic Games, **Jarome Iginla** scored two goals against the U.S. team to ensure Canada's gold-medal victory. This powerful forward was born in 1977 in Edmonton, Alberta, and is a top scorer in the NHL with a bright future.

Nova Scotia has produced many excellent Black boxers. **Sam Langford**, born in 1884 at Weymouth Falls, was a truly great heavyweight boxer. He held the heavyweight championships of England, Spain and Mexico — even though he was only 167 cm (5 ft. 6 in.) tall and weighed just 71 kg (157 lb.)!

"IT'S YOUR WORLD, SO TAKE PART IN IT AND NEVER GIVE UP ON YOUR DREAM."

— *Charmaine Crooks*

DID YOU KNOW

African immigrant **Daniel Igali** won Canada's first gold medal in wrestling at the Olympic Games in 2000. Igali was born in Nigeria in 1974, but in 1994 he left his 20 brothers and sisters behind to compete in the Commonwealth Games in Victoria, B.C. He stayed in Canada to train. When Igali won his Olympic gold medal, he joyfully kissed Canada's flag.

Ferguson Jenkins is a famous baseball player born in Chatham, Ontario, in 1943. A major-league pitcher, he struck out more than 3000 batters during his career with the Texas Rangers, the Chicago Cubs and the Boston Red Sox. In 1991, Jenkins was the first African Canadian inducted into the Baseball Hall of Fame.

The phrase "the real McCoy" comes from Black Canadian inventor **Elijah McCoy**. He was born in Canada in 1844, studied in Scotland, then moved to the United States. McCoy is most famous for inventing an automatic lubricator for train engines in 1882. He patented ideas for 50 different inventions, and his name came to stand for high-quality goods.

DANCER

PLAYWRIGHTS AND FILMMAKERS

Born in Barbados in 1960, **John Alleyne** studied ballet at the National Ballet School in Toronto. He became a popular solo dancer with Canada's National Ballet after joining the company in 1984. Alleyne then became a talented choreographer who created powerful new ballets. In 1992, this award-winning dancer was appointed artistic director of Ballet British Columbia.

Playwright **Djanet Sears** wrote Canada's first stage play by a person of African descent. Called *Afrika Solo*, it has been followed by many plays for adults and young people. Born in England, Sears moved with her family to Saskatoon, Saskatchewan, when she was 15. She has won many honours, including a Governor General's Award for *Harlem Duet* in 1998.

Clement Virgo, originally from Jamaica, moved to Canada when he was 11. He studied filmmaking at the Norman Jewison Canadian Film Centre, north of Toronto. The first film Virgo directed, *Rude*, won the Best Feature Film prize at the Toronto Film Festival. In 1997, he released his second full-length film, *The Planet of Junior Brown*.

OTHER BLACK CANADIAN FIRSTS

• **Leonard Braithwaite**, from Ontario, was the first Black person elected to Canada's Parliament.

• **George Dixon**, who was born in Nova Scotia, was the first Black person to win a World Boxing Championship, in 1890.

• **Jean Augustine**, of Ontario, was the first Black Canadian woman in Canada's Parliament and in the Cabinet (a group of advisers to the prime minister).

• **Anne Cools**, of Ontario, became Canada's first Black senator in 1984.

• **Willie O'Ree**, of New Brunswick, was the first Black NHL hockey player.

• **Corrine Sparks**, from Nova Scotia, was the first Black woman to become a judge in Canada, in 1987.

TIMELINE

3000 B.C.E.	The civilization of ancient Egypt begins in northern Africa
800 B.C.E.–300 C.E.	The kingdom of Kush flourishes south of Egypt
0–100 C.E.	Christianity reaches Africa
600s	After Muhammad's death, Islam spreads to northern Africa and beyond
800–1000	Africans develop trade routes within and beyond Africa
1000–1500	The medieval kingdoms of Ghana, Mali and Songhay flourish in western Africa
1000s	Swahili people build cities in eastern Africa
1200s	Zimbabwe Empire rises in southeast Africa
1492	Christopher Columbus's ships land on a Caribbean island
1497	The Italian explorer John Cabot lands in Newfoundland
1498	The Portuguese explorer Vasco da Gama is the first European to sail around Africa
1500s	Europeans set up plantations in the Caribbean and the Americas
1600–1850	During the Atlantic Slave Trade, millions of Africans are captured and sold to plantation owners
before 1605	Mathieu Da Costa is the first free Black person to set foot on Canadian soil
1608	French explorer Samuel de Champlain founds a colony at Quebec City
1628	Olivier Le Jeune, first enslaved Black person in New France, arrives in Quebec City
1709	France makes slavery legal in the colony of New France
1734	In Montreal, enslaved Black woman Marie-Joseph Angélique is hung for setting fire to her master's home
1760	Population of New France includes about 1200 enslaved Black people
1763	New France becomes a British colony called Quebec; slavery continues there
by 1767	American settlers and others have brought 100 enslaved Black people to Nova Scotia; a small number of slaves also live in Prince Edward Island (then Isle St. Jean)
1775–1783	Enslaved Black people from American southern states are promised freedom if they fight for Britain during the American Revolution
1777	Vermont becomes the first British colony to abolish slavery. Some enslaved Black people from Quebec escape there.
after 1783	Thirty-five hundred Black Loyalists and 1500 enslaved Black servants arrive in Nova Scotia and New Brunswick
1784	The Black Pioneers, an all-Black regiment, build Birchtown, Nova Scotia
1787	A colony where formerly enslaved Black people can live in freedom is established in Sierra Leone, Africa
1791	The Province of Quebec divides into Lower Canada and Upper Canada
1792	Twelve hundred Black Loyalists sail from Halifax to live in Sierra Leone
1793	Lieutenant-Governor John Graves Simcoe passes a law to limit slavery in Upper Canada
1796	Slave owner Peter Russell becomes governor of Upper Canada British government transports 600 Jamaican Maroons to Halifax, Nova Scotia
1800	Five hundred and fifty of the Jamaican Maroons sail to Sierra Leone

1812	War breaks out when America declares war on Britain and attacks Canada Richard Pierpoint, a Black Loyalist in Upper Canada, forms the Colored Corps Many American refugees join the fighting on the British/Canadian side
1814	Following the War of 1812, 2000 Black American war veterans settle in Nova Scotia and New Brunswick
1830	Josiah Henson escapes with his family and sets out for freedom in Canada
1831	The Underground Railroad gets rolling after a revolt by enslaved Black Americans led by Nat Turner
1834	Britain abolishes slavery in Canada and all other colonies
1841	Josiah Henson and family move to Dresden, Upper Canada Upper Canada becomes known as Canada West
1842	The Dawn Settlement is established by Josiah Henson
1849	William King establishes the Elgin Settlement near Chatham, Canada West
1850s	Harriet Tubman runs a "station" on the Underground Railroad in St. Catharines, Canada West
1850	In the U.S., the Fugitive Slave Act means enslaved Black people trying to escape can be hunted in free northern states About 60 000 free Black people have come to live in Canada West Canada West's Common Schools Act allows separate schools for Black and White children
1851	Mary Ann Shadd sets up an integrated school in Windsor, Canada West
1852	*Uncle Tom's Cabin*, a novel inspired by Josiah Henson's life, is published
1853	Mary Ann Shadd becomes the first Black woman to start a newspaper (the *Provincial Freeman*) in North America
1858	Four hundred families of Black Californians migrate to the new colony of Vancouver Island
1860	Black Californians form the all-Black Victoria Pioneer Rifle Company
1861	Civil War breaks out in the U.S. Thousands of Black Canadians join the Union (northern) army.
1863	In the U.S., President Lincoln passes the Emancipation Proclamation to free enslaved Black Americans. Black people in Canada are encouraged by this good news.
1865	The end of the Civil War brings the Underground Railroad to a close Slavery becomes illegal in the U.S. Some Black Americans who had come to Canada begin to return home.
1867	Confederation: Canada East (Quebec), Canada West (Ontario), New Brunswick and Nova Scotia join to create the Dominion of Canada The Reconstruction Act in the U.S. gives Blacks, including former enslaved Americans, equal rights with Whites
1867–1900	Over 30 000 Blacks return to the U.S. from Canada
1882	Black cowboy John Ware moves from Texas to Alberta
1905	Black American pioneers begin to settle in the Canadian Prairies
1909–1911	Fifteen hundred Exodusters from Oklahoma emigrate to the Canadian Prairies
1911–1912	A federal government regulation stops Black immigration
1914–1918	Only a few Black Canadians are allowed to fight as soldiers in World War I
1917	The all-Black No. 2 Construction Battalion sails for service in France

1919	Branches of Marcus Garvey's Universal Negro Improvement Association (now the Universal African Improvement Association) open in Canada Black porters form the first Canadian union that allows Black members
1930s	White and Black Canadians suffer in the Great Depression
1939–1945	Black Canadians fight in racially mixed units during World War II
1944	Ontario passes an act to prevent discrimination based on race or religion
1946	Nova Scotian writer Carrie Best publicizes discrimination against Blacks in cases such as Viola Desmond's
1954	In Ottawa, Black activists push for changes to the Immigration Act of 1952
1955	The Canadian Brotherhood of Sleeping Car Porters, a new union formed after World War II, wins Black porters the right to be promoted The Domestic Scheme encourages Caribbean women to come and work in Canada
1960s	Black Canadians join the civil rights movement in the U.S. The Black community of Africville, near Halifax, is destroyed
1962	A new Canadian Immigration Act prevents discrimination based on race or religion
1966	Black Canadians begin celebrating Kwanzaa
1967	Canada's points system aims to ensure equity and fairness for all immigrants The first Caribana parade is held in Toronto
1970s and 1980s	Thousands of Caribbean people become Canadian immigrants
1980s	Africans begin to emigrate directly to Canada
1983	Josiah Henson is the first African Canadian to appear on a Canadian stamp
1995	February is declared Black History Month across Canada

INDEX